W9-CJP-113

The War on
Terrorism

Other books in the Turning Points series:

Turning | Points
IN WORLD HISTORY

The War on Terrorism

Mitchell Young, *Book Editor*

Daniel Leone, *President*
Bonnie Szumski, *Publisher*
Scott Barbour, *Managing Editor*

GREENHAVEN
PRESS®

THOMSON

GALE

973.931
WAR

San Diego • Detroit • New York • San Francisco • Cleveland
New Haven, Conn. • Waterville, Maine • London • Munich

LIBRARY OF CONGRESS CATALOGING-IN-PUBLICATION DATA

The war on terrorism / Mitchell Young, book editor.
   p. cm. — (Turning points in world history)
Includes bibliographical references and index.
ISBN 0-7377-1470-0 (lib. : alk. paper) — ISBN 0-7377-1471-9 (pbk. : alk. paper)
  1. September 11 Terrorist Attacks, 2001. 2. War on Terrorism, 2001– .
3. Terrorism—United States—Prevention. 4. United States—Foreign relations—
Middle East. 5. World politics—1995–2005. I. Young, Mitchell. II. Turning points
in world history (Greenhaven Press)
HV6432.7 .W37 2003
973.931—dc21
                                             2002034717

Contents

Chapter 1: Events Leading Up to September 11

Chapter 2: Debating the War on Terrorism

reasons why so many people in the Middle East express hatred toward the United States.

Chapter 3: Domestic Antiterrorism Efforts

Chapter 4: The Next Phase: How Should the War Proceed?

Foreword

Certain past events stand out as pivotal, as having effects and outcomes that change the course of history. These events are often referred to as turning points. Historian Louis L. Snyder provides this useful definition:

> A turning point in history is an event, happening, or stage which thrusts the course of historical development into a different direction. By definition a turning point is a great event, but it is even more—a great event with the explosive impact of altering the trend of man's life on the planet.

History's turning points have taken many forms. Some were single, brief, and shattering events with immediate and obvious impact. The invasion of Britain by William the Conqueror in 1066, for example, swiftly transformed that land's political and social institutions and paved the way for the rise of the modern English nation. By contrast, other single events were deemed of minor significance when they occurred, only later recognized as turning points. The assassination of a little-known European nobleman, Archduke Franz Ferdinand, on June 28, 1914, in the Bosnian town of Sarajevo was such an event; only after it touched off a chain reaction of political-military crises that escalated into the global conflict known as World War I did the murder's true significance become evident.

Other crucial turning points occurred not in terms of a few hours, days, months, or even years, but instead as evolutionary developments spanning decades or even centuries. One of the most pivotal turning points in human history, for instance—the development of agriculture, which replaced nomadic hunter-gatherer societies with more permanent settlements—occurred over the course of many generations. Still other great turning points were neither events nor developments, but rather revolutionary new inventions and innovations that significantly altered social customs and ideas, military tactics, home life, the spread of knowledge, and the human condition in general. The developments of writing, gunpowder, the printing press, antibiotics, the electric light, atomic energy, television, and the computer, the last two of which have recently ushered in the world-altering information age, represent only some of these innovative turning points.

Each anthology in the Greenhaven Turning Points in World History series presents a group of essays chosen for their accessibility. The anthology's structure also enhances this accessibility. First, an introductory essay provides a general overview of the principal events and figures involved, placing the topic in its historical context. The essays that follow explore various aspects in more detail, some targeting political trends and consequences, others social, literary, cultural, and/or technological ramifications, and still others pivotal leaders and other influential figures. To aid the reader in choosing the material of immediate interest or need, each essay is introduced by a concise summary of the contributing writer's main themes and insights.

In addition, each volume contains extensive research tools, including a collection of excerpts from primary source documents pertaining to the historical events and figures under discussion. In the anthology on the French Revolution, for example, readers can examine the works of Rousseau, Voltaire, and other writers and thinkers whose championing of human rights helped fuel the French people's growing desire for liberty; the French *Declaration of the Rights of Man and Citizen*, presented to King Louis XVI by the French National Assembly on October 2, 1789; and eyewitness accounts of the attack on the royal palace and the horrors of the Reign of Terror. To guide students interested in pursuing further research on the subject, each volume features an extensive bibliography, which for easy access has been divided into separate sections by topic. Finally, a comprehensive index allows readers to scan and locate content efficiently. Each of the anthologies in the Greenhaven Turning Points in World History series provides students with a complete, detailed, and enlightening examination of a crucial historical watershed.

Introduction

The most successful terrorist event in history was carried out on September 11, 2001. In a series of coordinated attacks on the United States, Islamic terrorists claimed the lives of over three thousand people. The attacks destroyed billions of dollars in property. Billions more in economic losses were caused by the slowdown in economic activity in the days and weeks following the attack. More important than the economic losses, and perhaps even more significant than the tragic loss of life, was the damage that the terrorists inflicted on the most important symbols of American economic and military power.

The Plan

The terrorists' plan was straightforward: hijack four passenger jets and crash them into high profile targets in the United States. The nineteen operatives who carried out the attack were linked to al-Qaeda (the base), a terrorist network headed by wealthy Saudi Arabian exile Osama bin Laden. They succeeded in hijacking the four aircraft. Two of the hijacked planes were flown into the towers of the World Trade Center in New York City. One aircraft hit each tower. A third jet found its target in the Pentagon, the headquarters of the U.S. military, located in the Washington, D.C., area. The fourth plane is also thought to have been destined for Washington. It is believed that the passengers, alerted to the events of the day via cellular phones, prevented another successful attack by attempting to overpower the terrorists and regain control of the jet. During the ensuing struggle, the jetliner crashed into a field in rural Pennsylvania. Had not these passengers acted, it is likely the aircraft would have been crashed into a major government building in Washington.

Despite this one failure, in the eyes of al-Qaeda's leadership the attacks must have been a great success. Three of four teams of hijackers fulfilled their missions, and the fourth team was able to gain control of their target aircraft. Over three thousand American lives were lost, while only nineteen al-Qaeda members died in the attack. While the total cost of planning and executing the operation remains unknown, the property damage to the United States alone was surely hundreds of times greater than the expense of supporting the hijackers while they trained for their mission. But the greatest success of all was the symbolism of the attacks. The destruction of the towering skyscrapers in the heart of New York's—and the world's—financial center was a symbolic blow to America's economic might. The direct hit on the headquarters of the U.S. military was valuable as a demonstration of al-Qaeda's ability to strike the heart of American military power.

The propaganda value of the attacks was immediately evident. While Arab governments expressed sympathy for the American people, in the streets of Arab cities crowds marched to demonstrate their support for Osama bin Laden and his terrorist organization. In the West Bank, Palestinians danced and celebrated after hearing news of the attacks. Even in Europe and North America, most Muslim organizations were reluctant to criticize the attacks without adding that the United States had brought the attacks on itself through its aggressive and arrogant foreign policies in the Middle East.

The reaction in the Middle East was in stark contrast to the outpouring of sympathy and support from other parts of the world. In Europe, the governments of the North Atlantic Treaty Organization (NATO) quickly voted to support the United States militarily. In Europe, Canada, and the Pacific, citizens held candlelight vigils outside U.S. embassies. Tony Blair, the British prime minister, whose nation lost hundreds of citizens in the World Trade Center attack, flew to Washington to show his solidarity with the United States.

Americans, of course, were shocked and outraged at the attacks. The immediate task in New York and Washington was to rescue any survivors. It soon became apparent that there were few victims left alive under the rubble of the World Trade Center, and rescue efforts gave way to the grim task of recovering bodies.

The United States Launches the War on Terrorism

After a short period of national mourning, America found itself in an all-out war on terrorism. Addressing Congress and the nation on September 20, 2001, U.S. president George W. Bush declared that the new war was to be conducted on many fronts. A first step was to identify the organization behind the attacks. Investigators soon established the identity of the hijackers and searched their homes for evidence. The authorities also discovered there was a possible "twentieth hijacker," Zacarias Moussaoui, already in custody on immigration charges. Information found in the terrorists' residences and on Moussaoui's laptop computer linked the attacks to Osama bin Laden's al-Qaeda.

In addition to Moussaoui, hundreds of men of Middle Eastern origin were detained by federal officials and interrogated. Most of those detained were held on immigration charges, and the detentions raised concern among civil liberties and immigrants' rights groups. Islamic organizations and charities in the United States came under investigation for financially supporting terrorism, and a few of these organizations were shut down and had their assets seized.

These detentions were emblematic of a new attitude toward security taken by the U.S. government. The government tried to improve airport security, for example, by making all security screeners federal employees. Airline passengers were required to submit to more thorough inspections when boarding airplanes. New procedures were developed along the borders with Canada and Mexico in order to improve security while maintaining a reasonable rate of traffic flow.

Two far-reaching measures were adopted by Congress in order to fight terrorism on the domestic front. The USA Patriot Act, which was passed October 21, 2001, focused on enhancing the U.S. government's ability to conduct surveillance of terrorists, to track terrorists' financial assets, and to impose severe penalties for terrorism. The act also removed obstacles to information sharing among federal intelligence agencies. The Homeland Security Act, approved in July 2002, set up the Department of Homeland Security. This department was designed to coordinate the activities of various federal agencies—such as the FBI, the Immigration and Naturalization Service (INS), and the Coast Guard—involved in protecting the United States from another terrorist attack.

While the administration was pushing through legislation focusing on the domestic war on terrorism, it was also preparing to take the war to the terrorists. There was no doubt that the United States would retaliate for the attacks. Fortunately for the Bush administration, it had an identifiable target in Afghanistan. Afghanistan's Islamicist government, the Taliban, played host to Osama bin Laden. Al-Qaeda's terrorist training camps were also located in the landlocked Central Asian country. The Bush administration gave the Taliban an ultimatum: "Deliver to United States authorities all the leaders of al-Qaeda who hide in your land. . . . Hand over the terrorists, or . . . share in their fate." The Taliban refused to hand over bin Laden or the other al-

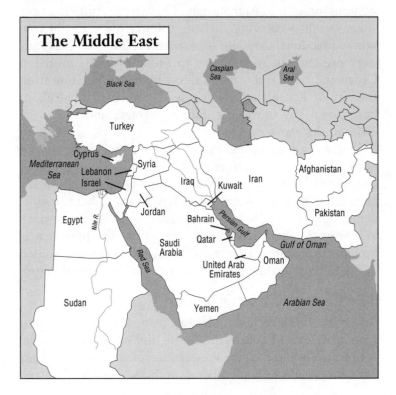

Qaeda leaders. President Bush decided military action was necessary. By October 2001, elite special forces soldiers were in Afghanistan to coordinate military operations with a local coalition of Afghans, called the Northern Alliance, who were fighting the Taliban.

The special forces in Afghanistan helped organize the Northern Alliance's military struggle against the Taliban. They also conducted intelligence operations. But their key role was in coordinating American air strikes against al-Qaeda and Taliban targets, which began on October 7. The Americans struck at strategic targets, such as al-Qaeda's training camps and its network of weapons storage areas. American warplanes also provided tactical air support to the Northern Alliance during its ground battles with Taliban forces. This air support shifted the balance of power to favor the rebels, and by December 7, 2001, most Taliban forces had been defeated.

The defeat of the Taliban led to the introduction of peace-keeping forces into Afghanistan. These forces not only provided stability, ensuring that the country did not split into warring factions, they also let Americans increase their military presence in Afghanistan in order to hunt down bin Laden and other important Taliban figures. Operating from the city of Khandahar, the United States began patrols to hunt down any remaining Taliban fighters and to restore order in the war-torn country.

Victory in Afghanistan came relatively quickly, but it did not end the war on terrorism. The United States captured hundreds of al-Qaeda soldiers and transported them to the U.S. naval base at Guantanamo Bay, Cuba. There, intelligence agents conducted interrogations of the prisoners. While no specifics have been released to the public, it is thought that information from Guantanamo prisoners aided in the foiling of some terrorist attacks on the United States.

The Causes of Islamic Terror

As the war on terror got underway, many commentators and scholars began to debate the causes and significance of the conflict. While the entire Western world, and much of East Asia, mourned the September 11 attacks, some in the Arab world and the larger Muslim world celebrated them. The differing reactions to the attacks underline what many analysts see as a basic division between the Islamic world and the Western world. These analysts see the Western world, meaning the democracies of Europe and North America, as being in conflict with those countries with Islamic governments or with overwhelmingly Muslim populations. According to this analysis, the West values free market capitalism and free trade, individual rights, and representative democracy. In contrast, Islamic societies are marked by respect for religion, traditional roles, and authoritarian regimes. Because of these two very different conceptions of a good society, neither side can understand the other.

According to Harvard political science professor Samuel Huntington, a "clash of civilizations" results when the West, through its technology and trade, spreads its culture into Islamic societies. Muslims in Saudi Arabia, for example, can watch MTV or the Disney Channel via satellite television. They can eat typical Western food at Pizza Hut or the McDonald's franchises. However, some Muslims object to this pervasive influence of Western culture. They see it as eroding the traditional values of their societies. Some Muslims are so opposed to this Western influence, they are willing to commit violence against what they believe to be the major source of this influence: the United States.

As evidence, supporters of the "clash of civilizations" view point out the series of attacks that have been committed by Islamic terrorists against westerners. For example, the September 11 attack was not the first time that terrorists targeted the World Trade Center. In 1993, Islamic terrorists exploded a van filled with explosives in a parking garage under the skyscrapers. The intent was to cause one tower to collapse, destroying the second tower as it fell. If the attack had succeeded, the loss of life would have been enormous. In 1997 Islamic terrorists machine-gunned a group of tourists in Egypt. In 1998 al-Qaeda bombed the U.S. embassies in Kenya and Tanzania. More attacks followed September 11 as well, including an attack on a French tanker off the coast of Yemen and the bombing of a disco, mainly filled with Australian young people, in Bali. Judging by the number of Islamic terrorist attacks on westerners, it would seem that those who believe that the West and Islam are in conflict have a good deal of evidence on their side.

Other analysts, however, say that Islamic terrorists do not represent the vast majority of Muslims. They point out that the central beliefs of Islam are not necessarily in conflict with Western values. According to this view, people in the Middle East desire Western goods, want to see Western movies, and listen to Western pop music. They also want Western-style democracy, but they are living under authoritarian regimes that suppress any campaigns for democracy. In the long run, these analysts believe, Muslims in the Middle East will be able to establish democratic governments and develop successful modern economies. Islamic terrorists are a handful of militant radicals who are fighting a losing battle against this inevitable modernization of Islamic societies.

A third view is that Islamic terrorists are reacting against specific U.S. policies in the Middle East. Islamic groups object to the United States's support for Israel, for example. Other complaints are the stationing of American troops on the "sacred land" of Saudi Arabia and the U.S.-led trade sanctions against Iraq, which have been blamed for the death of Iraqi children through malnutrition and lack of medicine. According to this analysis, Islamic terrorists have the goal of changing concrete U.S. policies rather than carrying out some abstract civilizational clash.

Islamic terrorists often attack U.S. military targets in the Middle East. They have attacked the Khobar Towers barracks in Saudi Arabia, killing nineteen U.S. Air Force personnel and wounding about five hundred. They also struck at an American warship, the USS *Cole*, killing seventeen U.S. sailors, while it was docked in Aden. Such attacks support the idea that the Islamic extremists are opposed to the specific policy of American military presence in the Middle East. Moreover, Osama bin Laden himself has claimed that his reasons for attacking the United States are American support for Israel in its struggle with the Palestinians and the presence of "infidel" troops in Saudi Arabia—home to

Mecca, the most holy of Islamic cities.

Other critics are quick to conclude that the terrorists themselves are solely to blame for the destruction they cause. To many, the notion that the terrorists are responding to the importation of U.S. culture or specific U.S. foreign policies is beside the point. The terrorists are the perpetrators of morally reprehensible acts—to speculate on their cause amounts to finding justifications for inexcusable acts.

Many believe that the true source of the violence is the distorted version of Islamic ideology adhered to by the terrorists. According to this belief system, Americans are infidels, so it is the adherent's duty to kill Americans and strive to bring about the destruction of the United States. As the September 11 attacks illustrate, many are willing to die for this cause. The reason that this relatively small number of people is able to generate so much destruction and terror stems from this zealous, absolutist mindset bent on the annihilation of their enemies regardless of the personal consequences.

How to Approach the War on Terror

These different analyses imply distinct ways of conducting the war on terrorism. If the "clash of civilizations" theory is correct, then it is perhaps best to try to avoid conflict with Islamic societies by minimizing the West's cultural and economic impact on the Middle East. Rather than advocating free trade and promoting democracy in the region, the United States should take a cautious approach. The impact of Western institutions on the region would be minimized to avoid provoking the wrath of Islamic fundamentalists. The emphasis would be on defensive measures to gather intelligence and prevent attacks, while realizing that people and governments in the region are not especially supportive of America.

On the other hand, if the people of the Islamic world truly want Western-style democracy and capitalism, the best approach might be to support groups in the region who are struggling for change. America could cooperate with regimes who are moderate in order to fight terrorism while influencing them to become more democratic. In the case of

Islamic or authoritarian governments who do not cooperate in the war on terrorism, the United States could support opposition groups who both promote democracy and support America in the fight against terror.

If Islamic terrorism is caused primarily by U.S. policy in the Middle East, however, it might be necessary to change that policy or face a long and difficult war on terrorism. Such changes might be a more balanced approach to the Israeli-Palestinian struggle, lifting of sanctions on Iraq, or even withdrawal of U.S. troops from Saudi Arabia and surrounding countries. These policy changes would be very difficult, however. The United States has long backed Israel as the only democracy in the region. In addition, many American voters have strong feelings about the necessity of supporting Israel against what they see as a Palestinian terror campaign to destroy the Jewish state. U.S. politicians would therefore face harsh criticism if they advocated withdrawing American support of Israel. The lifting of sanctions against Iraq is unlikely as long as Saddam Hussein is in power because he is seen as a dictator who is bent on obtaining weapons of mass destruction. The end of sanctions would mean that obtaining nuclear, biological, or chemical weapons would be easier for the Iraqi dictator. Nor is the withdrawal of American forces from the Middle East likely. The American military presence in the Persian Gulf and Saudi Arabia is seen as vital to maintaining stability in the Middle East, especially while Hussein still controls Iraq and its powerful army. It is unlikely that American troops and warships will leave the region any time soon.

Finally, if the terrorism is the work of extremist fanatics committed to the destruction of America, an offensive strategy, in line with Bush's war on terrorism, may be called for. In this case, disengaging from the Middle East or making subtle adjustments to foreign policy will have little effect. The United States will likely remain a target for deranged, suicidal followers of militant Islam. The most effective response is to go after the terrorists and prevent them from wreaking havoc by means of direct military action, covert operations, domestic and international surveillance, cutting off funding sources to terrorists, and even proactive military attacks against states thought to support terrorists, such as Iraq.

Foreign Policy Challenges and the War on Terrorism

As debate continues over the causes of terrorism and their corresponding remedies, the war on terrorism continues. The war in Afghanistan was won quickly and with few American losses, but trying to fight al-Qaeda members who have scattered to countries throughout the Islamic world will not be as simple as defeating the Taliban. The United States must carefully weigh its options, balancing the need for decisive and forceful action against the necessity of maintaining good relations with the Islamic world.

The United States and its Western allies will have to maintain good relations with more moderate Muslims throughout the world in order to win the war on terrorism. If the majority of Muslims harbor ill-will toward the West, terrorist organizations will be able to fill their ranks with new recruits. On the other hand, if most Muslims see the benefits in cooperating with the Western world, not only in issues of terrorism and security, but also in economic and cultural matters, they will have little reason to support any group or individual who endangers such cooperation.

A wider war on terror, particularly an attempt to topple the Iraqi dictator Saddam Hussein, may also lead to anti-American sentiment in the Middle East. In the past, Saddam had been condemned as a corrupt ruler by Islamic militants, including Osama bin Laden. But in the late 1990s, Saddam realized the value of being seen as a devout Muslim. His new devotion to religion, whether sincere or not, may play well among Muslims. If he is seen as a legitimate Islamic ruler being bullied by the superpower United States, American military action to remove him from power may backfire—despite its proposed potential to increase U.S. security and liberate oppressed Iraqi citizens.

In addition, the Palestinian-Israeli conflict—a continuing cycle of Palestinian terrorist attack and Israeli retaliation—presents a major challenge for U.S. policy makers. The U.S.

public generally supports Israel, and U.S. policy leans toward Israel. Many Muslims support the Palestinians, and believe that the United States must play a more even-handed role in the conflict. When it comes to this conflict, the president cannot ignore the feelings of Muslims throughout the world. The United States will need their cooperation in conducting the intelligence, law enforcement, and military operations necessary in the war on terrorism.

The Bush administration showed that it can engage in diplomacy in order to obtain the cooperation of the rulers of primarily Muslim nations in the war on terror. Particularly in Central Asia, a policy of intensive diplomacy led to closer U.S. ties with countries such as Uzbekistan and Tajikistan. This poor and potentially unstable area of the world is critical to further U.S. operations in Afghanistan. U.S. efforts in the region, both militarily and diplomatically, will remain a high priority. It is a matter of debate, however, just how long the intense involvement in the region will be necessary.

The Bush team has also increased U.S. ties to the Islamic government of Pakistan in order to secure its cooperation with the war. The situation in this South Asian country is more complex than that in Central Asia. Pakistan has a large Islamic fundamentalist movement. In fact, many al-Qaeda operatives studied at the *madrasas,* or Islamic religious schools, in Pakistan. It remains to be seen whether America's close relations with the Pakistani government will lead to popular support for the American-led war on terror within that nation.

The situation in Pakistan—good relations with the government but a tendency toward militant Islam among the people—is a problem that American policy makers face throughout the Middle East. The governments of both Saudi Arabia and Egypt have good relations with Washington. However, fifteen of nineteen September 11 hijackers were Saudi citizens, and Egypt has seen several acts of Islamic terrorism against Western tourists on its own soil. Clearly in both countries violent Islamic movements are a threat. Some analysts believe the threat should be met by continuing close ties with the region's governments while gently pressuring them to make democratic reforms. Others believe that the United States should promote rapid and radical change by supporting groups seeking democratic revolutions in Middle Eastern countries. Supporting groups seeking rapid change toward democracy would probably be too risky in Egypt or Saudi Arabia; the United States does not want to destabilize governments who are U.S. allies. In Iran, however, the United States might promote a revolt against a regime that is generally considered an enemy of America. This policy of "regime change" can be carried out through open support for democratic movements throughout the region or through secret (covert) support for those seeking to overthrow the existing governments in various Middle Eastern countries.

At the nongovernmental level, the United States faces the challenge convincing individual Muslims that it is not "the great Satan." While there is a strong anti-American and anti-Western element in the teachings of many Muslim clerics, there are also more tolerant varieties of Islam. Some scholars suggest seeing the world as a "clash of civilizations" ignores this more moderate side of Islam and only strengthens the hand of Islamic radicals. According to this analysis, the United States can foster a more moderate Islam through aid and dialogue. For example, the United States could fund nongovernmental organizations (NGOs) which are developing building or literacy programs in cooperation with local Islamic and secular institutions.

The Western, capitalist world might also be able to defeat Islamic terror by aiding trade and promoting prosperity in the Middle East. The theory here is that the hundreds of thousands of young men in the Middle East who have little prospect of decent employment make a fertile field for recruiting terrorists. Conversely, if these young men were employed and able to earn a decent wage, they would not be likely to risk their prosperity by joining in an anti-Western jihad (holy war). Contrary to this theory, most of the terrorists of September 11 were well educated and had experienced material success in the West, as had Osama bin Laden himself. Judging solely from the current evidence, it is quite possible that material prosperity aids in creating terrorists.

Defense or Engagement

A person's view of the correct policy in the war on terrorism will depend to a large extent on his or her view of the larger world. A view which sees a "clash of civilizations" will tend to lead toward a defensive position. The West must "keep its powder dry"; it must be prepared to defend itself from Islamic violence. According to this viewpoint, reaching out to moderate elements in Islam or forming alliances with the rulers of Islamic nations, while prudent at times, is not a reliable permanent policy against terror. The Islamic world is just too different; there are no grounds for long-lasting cooperation on policy.

On the other hand, if one sees Islam as a religion with many traditions, some tolerant and peaceful, others intolerant and violent, a policy of active engagement with the Islamic world is called for. The West should seek to strengthen moderate forms of Islam in order to undercut militant Islamicists on their own turf. Aid, economic development, and democratization will eventually lead to the end of Islamic terror. This result might even be sped along by promoting democratic revolutions in the Middle East. In the meantime, occasional military or law enforcement action will be necessary to prevent terrorists from attacking or punishing them when they do attack.

It is difficult to judge which of these arguments is correct. The first stages of the war on terror have shown that the United States and other Western countries can cooperate with parts of the Islamic world. The U.S.-led coalition of Western forces was able to cooperate with the Islamic rebels of the Northern Alliance to crush the Taliban and liberate Afghanistan. However, even though it has been damaged by the loss of its bases in Afghanistan, al-Qaeda has been able to continue its war of terror. Only the future will tell whether the war on terror is a battle with a fringe group of militant Islamic fundamentalists or part of an irremediable "clash of civilizations."

Chapter 1

Events Leading Up to September 11

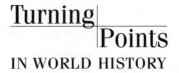

U.S. Policy in Afghanistan Created Conditions for the Growth of Terrorist Groups

Ahmed Rashid

In a book written before the September 11 attacks, Ahmed Rashid, a Central Asia correspondent for the *Far Eastern Economic Review* and the British newspaper *Daily Telegraph*, explores the connections between the United States Central Intelligence Agency (CIA), the Taliban, and Osama bin Laden. Specifically, he traces how CIA chief William Casey helped create the Mujaheddin, the forerunners of the Taliban, in order to fight the Soviet Union in Afghanistan, thus serving U.S. interests in the Cold War. However, the plan came back to haunt the United States, as the radical Islamicists the CIA helped to create turned against the West. The Taliban were aided by Muslims from all over the world, including Osama bin Laden. After the Soviets retreated from Afghanistan, the Taliban government gave bin Laden use of their territory to set up a terrorist organization, al-Qaeda, the group believed to be responsible for the September 11 attacks.

In 1986, [Central Intelligence Agency] chief William Casey had stepped up the war against the Soviet Union by taking three significant, but at that time highly secret, measures. He had persuaded the US Congress to provide the Mujaheddin [Islamic warriors] with American-made Stinger antiaircraft missiles to shoot down Soviet planes and provide US advisers to train the guerrillas. Until then no US-made weapons or personnel had been used directly in the war effort. The CIA, Britain's MI6 [Britain's Intelligence Agency]

Ahmed Rashid, *Militant Islam, Oil, and Fundamentalism in Central Asia*. New Haven, CT: Yale University Press, 2000. Copyright © 2000 by Ahmed Rashid. Reproduced by permission.

and the ISI [the Pakistani Inter-Services Intelligence Agency] also agreed on a provocative plan to launch guerrilla attacks into the Soviet Socialist Republics of Tajikistan and Uzbekistan, the soft Muslim underbelly of the Soviet state from where Soviet troops in Afghanistan received their supplies. The task was given to the ISI's favourite Mujaheddin leader Gulbuddin Hikmetyar. In March 1987, small units crossed the Amu Darya river from bases in northern Afghanistan and launched their first rocket attacks against villages in Tajikistan. Casey was delighted with the news and on his next secret trip to Pakistan he crossed the border into Afghanistan with President [Mohammed] Zia [-ul-Haq] to review the Mujaheddin groups.

Recruiting Radical Muslims

Thirdly, Casey committed CIA support to a long-standing ISI initiative to recruit radical Muslims from around the world to come to Pakistan and fight with the Afghan Mujaheddin. The ISI had encouraged this since 1982 and by now all the other players had their reasons for supporting the idea. President Zia aimed to cement Islamic unity, turn Pakistan into the leader of the Muslim world and foster an Islamic opposition in Central Asia. Washington wanted to demonstrate that the entire Muslim world was fighting the Soviet Union alongside the Afghans and their American benefactors. And the Saudis saw an opportunity both to promote Wahabbism [the faith of a strict Islamic sect] and get rid of its disgruntled radicals. None of the players reckoned on these volunteers having their own agendas, which would eventually turn their hatred against the Soviets on their own regimes and the Americans.

Pakistan already had standing instructions to all its embassies abroad to give visas, with no questions asked, to anyone wanting to come and fight with the Mujaheddin. In the Middle East, the Muslim Brotherhood, the Saudi-based World Muslim League and Palestinian Islamic radicals organized the recruits and put them into contact with the Pakistanis. The ISI and Pakistan's Jamaat-e-Islami [Islamic Party] set up reception committees to welcome, house and train the ar-

riving militants and then encouraged them to join the Mujaheddin groups, usually the Hizb-e-Islami [Party of Islam].
The funds for this enterprise came directly from Saudi Intelligence. French scholar Olivier Roy describes it as 'a joint
venture between the Saudis, the Muslim Brotherhood and
the Jamaat-e-Islami, put together by the ISI'.

Between 1982 and 1992 some 35,000 Muslim radicals
from 43 Islamic countries in the Middle East, North and
East Africa, Central Asia and the Far East would pass their
baptism under fire with the Afghan Mujaheddin. Tens of
thousands more foreign Muslim radicals came to study in
the hundreds of new *madrassas* [Islamic schools] that Zia's
military government began to fund in Pakistan and along the
Afghan border. Eventually more than 100,000 Muslim radicals were to have direct contact with Pakistan and Afghanistan and be influenced by the jihad.

In camps near [the Pakistani border city of] Peshawar and
in Afghanistan, these radicals met each other for the first
time and studied, trained and fought together. It was the first
opportunity for most of them to learn about Islamic movements in other countries and they forged tactical and ideological links that would serve them well in the future. The
camps became virtual universities for future Islamic radicalism. None of the intelligence agencies involved wanted to
consider the consequences of bringing together thousands
of Islamic radicals from all over the world. 'What was more
important in the world view of history? The Taliban or the
fall of the Soviet Empire? A few stirred-up Muslims or the
liberation of Central Europe and the end of the Cold War?'
said Zbigniew Brzezinski, a former US National Security
Adviser. American citizens only woke up to the consequences when Afghanistan-trained Islamic militants blew up
the World Trade Centre in New York in 1993, killing six
people and injuring 1,000.

Creating an Enemy

'The war,' wrote Samuel Huntington, 'left behind an uneasy
coalition of Islamist organizations intent on promoting
Islam against all non-Muslim forces. It also left a legacy of

expert and experienced fighters, training camps and logistical facilities, elaborate trans-Islam networks of personal and organization relationships, a substantial amount of military equipment including 300 to 500 unaccounted-for Stinger missiles, and, most important, a heady sense of power and self-confidence over what had been achieved and a driving desire to move on to other victories.'

Most of these radicals speculated that if the Afghan jihad had defeated one superpower, the Soviet Union, could they not also defeat the other superpower, the US and their own regimes? The logic of this argument was based on the simple premise that the Afghan jihad alone had brought the Soviet state to its knees. The multiple internal reasons which led to the collapse of the Soviet system, of which the jihad was only one, were conveniently ignored. So while the USA saw the collapse of the Soviet state as the failure of the communist system, many Muslims saw it solely as a victory for Islam. For militants this belief was inspiring and deeply evocative of the Muslim sweep across the world in the seventh and eighth centuries. A new Islamic *Ummah* [the community of all true believers in Islam], they argued, could be forged by the sacrifices and blood of a new generation of martyrs and more such victories.

Amongst these thousands of foreign recruits was a young Saudi student Osama Bin Laden, the son of a Yemeni construction magnate Mohammed Bin Laden who was a close friend of the late King Faisal and whose company had become fabulously wealthy on the contracts to renovate and expand the Holy Mosques of Mecca and Medina. The ISI had long wanted Prince Turki Bin Faisal, the head of *Istakhbarat*, the Saudi Intelligence Service, to provide a Royal Prince to lead the Saudi contingent in order to show Muslims the commitment of the Royal Family to the jihad. Only poorer Saudis, students, taxi-drivers and Bedouin tribesmen had so far arrived to fight. But no pampered Saudi Prince was ready to rough it out in the Afghan mountains. Bin Laden, although not a royal, was close enough to the royals and certainly wealthy enough to lead the Saudi contingent. Bin Laden, Prince Turki and [Lieutenant General Hameed

Gul, the head of the ISI] were to become firm friends and allies in a common cause.

The Arab-Afghans

The centre for the Arab-Afghans was the offices of the World Muslim League and the Muslim Brotherhood in Peshawar which was run by Abdullah Azam, a Jordanian Palestinian whom Bin Laden had first met at university in Jeddah and revered as his leader. Azam and his two sons were assassinated by a bomb blast in Peshawar in 1989. During the 1980s Azam had forged close links with Hikmetyar and Abdul Rasul Sayyaf, the Afghan Islamic scholar, whom the Saudis had sent to Peshawar to promote Wahabbism. Saudi funds flowed to Azam and the Makhtab al Khidmat or Services Centre which he created in 1984 to service the new recruits and receive donations from Islamic charities. Donations from Saudi Intelligence, the Saudi Red Crescent, the World Muslim League and private donations from Saudi princes and mosques were channelled through the Makhtab. A decade later the Makhtab would emerge at the centre of a web of radical organizations that helped carry out the World Trade Centre bombing and the bombings of US Embassies in Africa in 1998.

Until he arrived in Afghanistan, Bin Laden's life had hardly been marked by anything extraordinary. He was born around 1957, the 17th of 57 children sired by his Yemeni father and a Saudi mother, one of Mohammed Bin Laden's many wives. Bin Laden studied for a Masters degree in business administration at King Abdul Aziz University in Jeddah but soon switched to Islamic studies. Thin and tall, he is six feet five inches, with long limbs and a flowing beard, he towered above his contemporaries who remember him as a quiet and pious individual but hardly marked out for greater things.

His father backed the Afghan struggle and helped fund it, so when Bin Laden decided to join up, his family responded enthusiastically. He first travelled to Peshawar in 1980 and met the Mujaheddin leaders, returning frequently with Saudi donations for the cause until 1982 when he decided to settle in Peshawar. He brought in his company engineers and heavy construction equipment to help build roads and depots for the Mujaheddin. In 1986 he helped build the Khost tunnel complex, which the CIA was funding as a major arms storage depot, training facility and medical centre for the Mujaheddin, deep under the mountains close to the Pakistan border. For the first time in Khost he set up his own training camp for Arab Afghans, who now increasingly saw this lanky, wealthy and charismatic Saudi as their leader. . . .

Infidels in Saudi Arabia

By 1990 Bin Laden was disillusioned by the internal bickering of the Mujaheddin and he returned to Saudi Arabia to work in the family business. He founded a welfare organization for Arab-Afghan veterans, some 4,000 of whom had settled in Mecca and Medina alone, and gave money to the families of those killed. After Iraq's invasion of Kuwait he lobbied the Royal Family to organize a popular defence of the Kingdom and raise a force from the Afghan war veterans to fight Iraq. Instead King Fahd invited in the Americans. This came as an enormous shock to Bin Laden. As the 540,000 US troops began to arrive, Bin Laden openly criticized the Royal Family, lobbying the Saudi *ulema* [Islamic religious leaders] to issue fatwas, religious rulings, against non-Muslims being based in the country.

Bin Laden's criticism escalated after some 20,000 US troops continued to be based in Saudi Arabia after Kuwait's liberation. In 1992 he had a fiery meeting with Interior Minister Prince Naif whom he called a traitor to Islam. Naif complained to King Fahd and Bin Laden was declared persona non grata. Nevertheless he still had allies in the Royal Family, who also disliked Naif while he maintained his links with both Saudi Intelligence and the ISI.

In 1992 Bin Laden left for Sudan to take part in the Islamic revolution underway there under the charismatic Sudanese leader Hassan Turabi. Bin Laden's continued criticism of the Saudi Royal Family eventually annoyed them so much that they took the unprecedented step of revoking his citizenship in 1994. It was in Sudan, with his wealth and contacts that Bin Laden gathered around him more veterans of the Afghan war, who were all disgusted by the American victory over Iraq and the attitude of the Arab ruling elites who allowed the US military to remain in the Gulf. As US and Saudi pressure mounted against Sudan for harbouring Bin Laden, the Sudanese authorities asked him to leave.

In May 1996 Bin Laden travelled back to Afghanistan, arriving in Jalalabad in a chartered jet with an entourage of dozens of Arab militants, bodyguards and family members including three wives and 13 children. Here he lived under the protection of the Jalalabad Shura until the conquest of Kabul and Jalalabad by the Taliban in September 1996. In August 1996 he had issued his first declaration of jihad against the Americans whom he said were occupying Saudi Arabia. 'The walls of oppression and humiliation cannot be demolished except in a rain of bullets,' the declaration read. Striking up a friendship with Mullah Omar, in 1997 he moved to Kandahar and came under the protection of the Taliban.

Tracking Bin Laden

By now the CIA had set up a special cell to monitor his activities and his links with other Islamic militants. A US State Department report in August 1996 noted that Bin Laden was 'one of the most significant financial sponsors of Islamic extremist activities in the world'. The report said that Bin Laden was financing terrorist camps in Somalia, Egypt, Sudan, Yemen, Egypt and Afghanistan. In April 1996, President Clinton signed the Anti-Terrorism Act which allowed the US to block assets of terrorist organizations. It was first used to block Bin Laden's access to his fortune of an estimated US$250–300 million. A few months later Egyptian intelligence declared that Bin Laden was training 1,000 militants, a second generation of Arab-Afghans, to bring about an Islamic revolution in Arab countries.

In early 1997 the CIA constituted a squad which arrived in Peshawar to try and carry out a snatch operation to get Bin Laden out of Afghanistan. The Americans enlisted Afghans and Pakistanis to help them but aborted the operation. The US activity in Peshawar helped persuade Bin Laden to move to the safer confines of Kandahar. On 23

February 1998, at a meeting in the original Khost camp, all the groups associated with Al Qaeda issued a manifesto under the aegis of 'The International Islamic Front for jihad against Jews and Crusaders'. The manifesto stated 'for more than seven years the US has been occupying the lands of Islam in the holiest of places, the Arabian peninsular, plundering its riches, dictating to its rulers, humiliating its people, terrorizing its neighbours, and turning its bases in the peninsular into a spearhead through which to fight the neighbouring Muslim peoples'.

The meeting issued a fatwa. 'The ruling to kill the Americans and their allies—civilians and military—is an individual duty for every Muslim who can do it in any country in which it is possible to.' Bin Laden had now formulated a policy that was not just aimed at the Saudi Royal Family or the Americans but called for the liberation of the entire Muslim Middle East. As the American air war against Iraq escalated in 1998, Bin Laden called on all Muslims to 'confront, fight and kill' Americans and Britons.

However, it was the bombings in August 1998 of the US Embassies in Kenya and Tanzania that killed 220 people which made Bin Laden a household name in the Muslim world and the West. Just 13 days later, after accusing Bin Laden of perpetrating the attack, the USA retaliated by firing 70 cruise missiles against Bin Laden's camps around Khost and Jalalabad. Several camps which had been handed over by the Taliban to the Arab-Afghans and Pakistani radical groups were hit. The Al Badr camp controlled by Bin Laden and the Khalid bin Walid and Muawia camps run by the Pakistani Harakat ul Ansar were the main targets. Harakat used their camps to train militants for fighting Indian troops in Kashmir. Seven outsiders were killed in the strike—three Yemenis, two Egyptians, one Saudi and one Turk. Also killed were seven Pakistanis and 20 Afghans.

In November 1998 the USA offered a US$5-million reward for Bin Laden's capture. The Americans were further galvanized when Bin Laden claimed that it was his Islamic duty to acquire chemical and nuclear weapons to use against the USA. 'It would be a sin for Muslims not to try to possess the weapons that would prevent infidels from inflicting harm on Muslims. Hostility towards America is a religious duty and we hope to be rewarded for it by God,' he said. . . .

Jihad Worldwide

The Clinton administration was desperately looking for a diversion as it wallowed through the mire of the Monica Lewinsky affair and also needed an all-purpose, simple explanation for unexplained terrorist acts. Bin Laden became the centre of what was promulgated by Washington as a global conspiracy against the USA. What Washington was not prepared to admit was that the Afghan jihad, with the support of the CIA, had spawned dozens of fundamentalist movements across the Muslim world which were led by militants who had grievances, not so much against the Americans, but their own corrupt, incompetent regimes. As early as 1992–93 Egyptian and Algerian leaders at the highest level had advised Washington to re-engage diplomatically in Afghanistan in order to bring about peace so as to end the presence of the Arab-Afghans. Washington ignored the warnings and continued to ignore Afghanistan even as the civil war there escalated.

The Algerians were justified in their fears, for the first major eruption from the ranks of the Arab-Afghans came in Algeria. In 1991 the Islamic Salvation Front (FIS) won the first round of parliamentary elections taking some 60 per cent of the seats countrywide. The Algerian army cancelled the results, declared Presidential rule in January 1992 and within two months a vicious civil war began which had claimed some 70,000 lives by 1999. FIS itself was outmanoeuvered by the more extreme Islamic Jihad, which in 1995 changed its name to the Armed Islamic Group (GIA). GIA was led by Algerian Afghans—Algerian veterans from the Afghan war—who were neo-Wahabbis and set an agenda that was to plunge Algeria into a bloodbath, destabilize North Africa and lead to the growth of Islamic extremism in France. Algeria was only a foretaste of what was to come later. Bombings carried out in Egypt by Islamic groups were also traced back to Egyptian veterans trained in Afghanistan.

Bin Laden knew many of the perpetrators of these violent acts across the Muslim world, because they had lived and fought together in Afghanistan. His organization, focused around supporting veterans of the Afghan war and their families, maintained contacts with them. He may well have funded some of their operations, but he was unlikely to know what they were all up to or what their domestic agendas were. Bin Laden has always been insecure within the architecture of Islam. He is neither an Islamic scholar nor a teacher and thus cannot legally issue fatwas although he does so. In the West his 'Death to America' appeals have been read as fatwas, even though they do not carry moral weight in the Muslim world.

Arab-Afghans who knew him during the jihad say he was neither intellectual nor articulate about what needed to be done in the Muslim world. In that sense he was neither the Lenin of the Islamic revolution, nor was he the internationalist ideologue of the Islamic revolution such as Che Guevara was to revolution in the third world. . . .

Bin Laden Behind Bombing of U.S. Embassies in Africa

After the August 1998 Africa bombings, US pressure on the Saudis increased. Prince Turki visited Kandahar again, this time to persuade the Taliban to hand over Bin Laden. In their meeting, Mullah Omar refused to do so and then insulted Prince Turki by abusing the Saudi Royal Family. Bin Laden himself described what took place. 'He [Prince Turki] asked Mullah Omar to surrender us home or to expel us from Afghanistan. It is none of the business of the Saudi regime to come and ask for the handing over of Osama Bin Laden. It was as if Turki came as an envoy of the American government. Furious about the Taliban insults, the Saudis suspended diplomatic relations with the Taliban and ostensibly ceased all aid to them, although they did not withdraw recognition of the Taliban government.

By now Bin Laden had developed considerable influence with the Taliban, but that had not always been the case. The Taliban's contact with the Arab-Afghans and their Pan-

Islamic ideology was non-existent until the Taliban captured Kabul in 1996. Pakistan was closely involved in introducing Bin Laden to the Taliban leaders in Kandahar, because it wanted to retain the Khost training camps for Kashmiri militants, which were now in Taliban hands. Persuasion by Pakistan, the Taliban's better-educated cadres, who also had Pan-Islamic ideas, and the lure of financial benefits from Bin Laden, encouraged the Taliban leaders to meet with Bin Laden and hand him back the Khost camps.

Partly for his own safety and partly to keep control over him, the Taliban shifted Bin Laden to Kandahar in 1997. At first he lived as a paying guest. He built a house for Mullah Omar's family and provided funds to other Taliban leaders. He promised to pave the road from Kandahar airport to the city and build mosques, schools and dams but his civic works never got started as his funds were frozen. While Bin Laden lived in enormous style in a huge mansion in Kandahar with his family, servants and fellow militants, the arrogant behaviour of the Arab-Afghans who arrived with him and their failure to fulfil any of their civic projects, antagonized the local population. The Kandaharis saw the Taliban leaders as beneficiaries of Arab largesse rather than the people.

Bin Laden endeared himself further to the leadership by sending several hundred Arab-Afghans to participate in the 1997 and 1998 Taliban offensives in the north. These Wahabbi fighters helped the Taliban carry out the massacres of the Shia Hazaras in the north. Several hundred Arab-Afghans, based in the Rishkor army garrison outside Kabul, fought on the Kabul front. . . . Increasingly, Bin Laden's world view appeared to dominate the thinking of senior Taliban leaders. All-night conversations between Bin Laden and the Taliban leaders paid off. Until his arrival the Taliban leadership had not been particularly antagonistic to the USA or the West but demanded recognition for their government.

However, after the Africa bombings the Taliban became increasingly vociferous against the Americans, the UN, the Saudis and Muslim regimes around the world. Their statements increasingly reflected the language of defiance Bin Laden had adopted and which was not an original Taliban

trait. As US pressure on the Taliban to expel Bin Laden intensified, the Taliban said he was a guest and it was against
Afghan tradition to expel guests. When it appeared that
Washington was planning another military strike against Bin
Laden, the Taliban tried to cut a deal with Washington—to
allow him to leave the country in exchange for US recognition. Thus until the winter of 1998 the Taliban saw Bin
Laden as an asset, a bargaining chip over whom they could
negotiate with the Americans.

The US State Department opened a satellite telephone
connection to speak to Mullah Omar directly. The Afghanistan desk officers, helped by a Pushto translator, held
lengthy conversations with Omar in which both sides explored various options, but to no avail. By early 1999 it
began to dawn on the Taliban that no compromise with the
US was possible and they began to see Bin Laden as a liabil-
ity. A US deadline in February 1999 to the Taliban to either
hand over Bin Laden or face the consequences forced the
Taliban to make him disappear discreetly from Kandahar.
The move bought the Taliban some time, but the issue was
still nowhere near being resolved.

The Arab-Afghans had come full circle. From being mere
appendages to the Afghan jihad and the Cold War in the
1980s they had taken centre stage for the Afghans, neighbouring countries and the West in the 1990s. The USA was
now paying the price for ignoring Afghanistan between 1992
and 1996, while the Taliban were providing sanctuary to the
most hostile and militant Islamic fundamentalist movement
the world faced in the post–Cold War era. Afghanistan was
now truly a haven for Islamic internationalism and terrorism
and the Americans and the West were at a loss as to how to
handle it.

U.S. Military and Economic Power Caused Resentment Among Muslims

Paul R. Pillar

In the aftermath of the September 11 attacks, many Americans asked what caused some Muslims to so hate the United States and the West that they would kill themselves and murder thousands of civilians in unprecedented terrorist attacks. In the following excerpt written shortly before the attacks, Paul R. Pillar, a former deputy chief of the Counterterrorist Center at the Central Intelligence Agency, writes that the primary cause of Islamic resentment toward the United States stems from America's status as the world's most powerful country. Other reasons include America's support of regimes that are unfriendly toward radical Islam—especially Israel—and a culture that is deemed decadent and destructive of Islamic values. Western economic and military power is too great to confront head-on; unable to counter the United States by conventional military tactics, these extremist groups turn to terrorism.

The special place that the United States occupies on terrorists' hit lists reflects more than just the efficacy of terrorism as a weapon of the weak or the number and accessibility of potential U.S. targets. It also is a product of the special resentment that terrorists hold toward the United States. Terrorists strike this country so often not just because they are able to, but because they want to. Both the operations and the rhetoric of the terrorists make this clear.

This leads to the question of why the resentment exists

Paul R. Pillar, *Terrorism and U.S. Foreign Policy*. Washington, DC: Brookings Institution Press, 2001. Copyright © 2001 by The Brookings Institution. Reproduced by permission.

and what if anything could be done to lessen it. Does the hatred stem from what the United States *does* (which presumably could be changed) or from what it *is* (which is far less alterable)? Some have suggested that the extent of U.S. activity overseas—particularly in certain areas such as the Middle East—underlies the resentment, implying that curtailment of this activity would mean less resentment and hence less terrorism. The truth, as with most truths about terrorism (even confining one's purview to the radical Islamists), is that a mixture of factors is at work. Terrorist hatred involves both the actions and the essence of the United States. Some of the actions, however, are almost intrinsic to being a superpower, and terrorists' sentiments about all of the actions are shaped by their larger, long-standing hatred of U.S. power and what they associate with that power. More than anything else, it is the United States' predominant place atop the world order (with everything that implies militarily, economically, and culturally) and the perceived U.S. opposition to change in any part of that order that underlie terrorists' resentment of the United States and their intent to attack it.

Terrorists do often respond to specific initiatives or interventions overseas, particularly ones involving military force. The intervention could be anything from a retaliatory strike such as the bombing of Libya in 1986 to a primarily humanitarian operation such as Operation Restore Hope in Somalia in 1992–94. Typically there is a burst of small-scale attacks following such an event, partly out of genuine sympathy for the perceived victims of the operation and partly because the event provides an excuse for doing something against the United States. The intervention then becomes an oft-cited grievance that plays a part in the rationales for later, possibly larger, attacks. The Somalia operation was specifically mentioned in a statement that bin Ladin's International Islamic Front for Holy War against Jews and Crusaders issued several days after the East Africa bombings. The U.S. embassies in Nairobi [Kenya] and Dar es Salaam [Tanzania], according to the Islamic Front's statement, were appropriate targets because they had "supervised the killings of at least 13,000 Somali civilians in the treacherous attack led by America against this Muslim country." The actual selection of those embassies as targets probably had more to do with the feasibility of operating in Kenya and Tanzania (given local infrastructures and perceived vulnerability of the targets) than the earlier events in Somalia. Nonetheless, Restore Hope was a genuine issue. Many in the Middle East thought it had more to do with colonialism than with humanitarianism. The mission creep that characterized Restore Hope—in which what started as a humanitarian operation later involved a hunt for Somali warlord Mohamed Farrah Aideed—encouraged such perceptions.

U.S. ties to governments that the extremists hate is another reason the extremists hate the United States. The friend of one's enemy is itself seen as an enemy. U.S. friendship with the Saudi government and with moderate Arab leaders such as Egypt's Hosni Mubarak has been part of this perspective. The relationship that terrorists invoke far more than any other, however, is that between the United States and Israel. The claim of responsibility for the Africa bombings made by bin Ladin's paper front, the "Islamic Army for the Liberation of the Holy Shrines," included a demand for an end to "all American support to Israel." The Islamists (and many less extreme Muslims) look on Israel as a successor to the Crusader states: a creature imposed by the West that has displaced the native civilization and culture. The leader of the Tunisian Islamist movement, Rashid Ghannushi, has said that "Israel represents the projection of this [Western] center into the East to wipe out its specific character, its spiritual wealth." The U.S. role in this picture is both as the current leader of the West that established this Zionist beachhead in the Muslim world and as the principal military supplier and backer of Israel. On the military side, the United States is thus implicated in such events as the humiliating Arab defeat in the Six-Day War of 1967, which radicalized the Islamist movement more than any earlier events and that still, a third of a century later, remains seared in the consciousness of many Muslims and in particular many Arabs.

U.S. Military Presence Is a Cause of Terrorism

Besides specific interventions and ties to hated governments, the mere presence of U.S. contingents overseas is an ingredient in terrorist resentment against the United States. This is especially true of a military presence, that most direct and forceful manifestation of U.S. power. The major terrorist bombings in Lebanon in the 1980s were stimulated by, and intended to end, the presence of U.S. and allied forces there, as well as scuttling a U.S.-led peace process. Expulsion of the U.S. military from the Arabian Peninsula has now become a similar cause, though one that the terrorists have found harder to achieve.

Bin Ladin in particular has focused on the U.S. military presence in his former homeland. In a letter he sent to an Arabic-language newspaper in London in 1996, he said it was the "legitimate right" of Saudis to strike at the 5,000 American troops stationed in Saudi Arabia, even though King Fahd had invited them. The claim by the "Islamic Army for the Liberation of the Holy Shrines" included as one of its demands "evacuation of U.S. and western forces from the Islamic countries in general and the Arabian Peninsula in particular." If bin Ladin's organization could have struck those forces directly they undoubtedly would have done so, but that would have been less feasible (particularly given the security-driven U.S. redeployment following Khubar Towers [a 1996 terrorist attack in Saudi Arabia that killed 19 and wounded 515]) than hitting embassies in a couple of African capitals.

The presence of U.S. troops in the kingdom angers the likes of bin Ladin in two ways. First, it is seen as a prop holding up the Saudi royal regime. Second, there is the more symbolic concern (implied by the reference to Holy Shrines in the "Islamic Army's" name) of foreign troops staying in the land most sacred to Islam. American boots are seen as contaminating the soil on which the Prophet walked.

A diplomatic presence is less controversial than a military one; overseas diplomatic representation is, after all, a normal attribute of statehood. But embassies can also become symbols—especially big, highly visible embassies, of which the

United States has more than anyone else. The accusations against the U.S. embassies in Nairobi and Dar es Salaam in the World Islamic Front's statement plays to an old theme of embassies being centers of machination—or "nests of spies," as the U.S. embassy in Tehran was described when it was seized [in 1979]. The front's statement contained the demand that all U.S. embassies in Muslim lands be closed and their employees expelled.

Opposition to Spread of U.S. Commerce and Culture

The U.S. commercial and cultural presence overseas—although it cannot be linked as directly to U.S. policies as diplomatic or military installations can—has also been the target of terrorism conducted solely for reasons of symbolism and hatred (as distinct from more instrumental uses of terrorism such as hostage taking, in which U.S. business has also figured as a target). Leftists, for example, have frequently struck U.S.-owned business as blows against "economic imperialism." Attacks by Greek leftists in 1999 alone included hits against offices of American Express and Chase Manhattan, a General Motors dealership, and a McDonald's. Similarly, when the Tupac Amaru Revolutionary Movement (MRTA) in Peru was still active and capable, it repeatedly attacked American-affiliated enterprises, including branches of Citibank, Kentucky Fried Chicken, and Pizza Hut.

This is where the sources of terrorist resentment against the United States get less into what it does and more into what it is. Very few of the attacks against U.S.-owned businesses in Greece or Peru were stimulated by any particular U.S. initiatives or policies. A branch office of Citibank or a McDonald's restaurant just happens to be among the more accessible, tangible, and attackable manifestations of a much larger U.S.-dominated culture and economy that is the main object of scorn and anger. Other manifestations to which the foreign extremists are exposed include American-made or -inspired goods and services, a largely American-created mass culture, and mass media through which the goods are advertised and the culture is conveyed. Globalization has increased the exposure to each of these. And the reactions to each of these—including the hostile reactions of extremists—are responses not just to the substance of the object at hand (the good, the service, the branch office, and so forth) but to the kind of America the object represents. As Benjamin Barber has observed about U.S. corporations marketing consumer goods overseas, "Selling American products means selling America: its popular culture, its putative prosperity, its ubiquitous imagery and software, and thus its very soul. Merchandising is as much about symbols as about goods and sells not life's necessities but life's styles."

The leftists have opposed this America violently because to them it is the font of economic exploitation. The Islamists oppose it violently because to them it is the font of a torrent of dirty water that is polluting the pond where they live. There is so much about American culture for the Islamists to hate, from its overall materialism to the role of women to the more sensual aspects of popular entertainment. And the cultural torrent is not only polluting the pond, it is making waves that are destroying old and fragile structures that were built along it. The American-originated changes in what people throughout the Muslim world are seeing and hearing, on the airwaves and on street corners, is tearing down mores on the obedience of children, the relationship between the sexes, and much else. The Islamists see these changes as wrecking a traditional social fabric without putting anything in its place that offers self-respect and stability, or even—for most Muslims—a more prosperous life.

Stereotypes Damage U.S. Image

The face of America that much of the world sees through the global mass media is not its best face. It is a face that reinforces some of the worst stereotypes that Islamists hold about the United States. News coverage that naturally focuses on troubles rather than good news can easily leave an impression of an America that is dominated by racism, drug abuse, the breakdown of families, and other societal ills. American popular entertainment, especially some forms of popular music, appalls the Islamists even more. The more debauched parts of this ubiquitous segment of American culture have been targets of social critics in the United States. It should not be surprising that the revulsion an Islamic fundamentalist feels is even greater, to the point in some cases of contributing to a predisposition toward anti-American violence. Many Islamists take the popular entertainment to be truly representative of the United States. A Pakistani fundamentalist group, for example, denounced two stars of American pop music, Michael Jackson and Madonna, as "the torchbearers of American society, their cultural and social values . . . that are destroying humanity. They are ruining the lives of thousands of Muslims and leading them to destruction, away from their religion, ethics, and morality." The group said the two entertainers are "cultural terrorists" who should be brought to trial in Pakistan.

There are, to be sure, countervailing elements in American culture—evoking prosperity and freedom—that have been an attractive rather than a repellent force in much of the world, including the Muslim world. The U.S. dominance both of a propagating culture and of global media that convey it is a source of U.S. influence—part of what Joseph Nye [professor of public policy at Harvard] has called "soft power." But the Islamists and other religious extremists focus more on the negative aspects, not only because of the distorting effects of the media lens but because of the impact on those imperiled aspects of their own culture that are most important to them. Besides, the very U.S. dominance of global media is another form of resented U.S. power, as well as another reason for terrorists bent on gaining maximum publicity to attack U.S. targets. And succumbing to the lure of Western consumer goods does not remove hatred of the society that produced them. As [Samuel] Huntington [political science professor at Harvard] has colorfully put it, "Somewhere in the Middle East a half-dozen young men could well be dressed in jeans, drinking Coke, listening to rap, and, between their bows to Mecca, putting together a bomb to blow up an American airliner." The music may be the Muslim version of rap, but the scene is not altogether implausible.

Most of the Islamists' animus toward the United States

does not reflect tenets of Islam (even the more fundamentalist interpretations of them) as it does a more general religious self-righteousness confronting secularism. Islamists share with the extremists of other religions a view of themselves as part of a cosmic struggle, with their religious belief giving a moral sanction to violence. It is a common trait of all such extremists that they deem the lives of individuals who may die in the course of battling a cosmic enemy (including ones who die in terrorist attacks) to be of little importance. Certain aspects of the Islamic world view do, however, lend themselves more than other belief systems to the notion of an inevitable and violent clash with the U.S.-led West. The division of the world in this view between Dar al-Islam (The Realm of Islam) and Dar al-Harb (The Realm of War), the obligation of Muslims to try to expand the faith (the idea of jihad), and the lack of a clear distinction between temporal and spiritual matters all contribute to this. These and other tenets of Islam are subject to multitudinous interpretations, and for the great majority of Muslims they do not dictate violence, let alone terrorism. Jihad can take many peaceful forms. That is why Huntington's concept of a religiously based clash does not describe the interactions that most Muslims, and most Muslim states and organizations, have with the United States and the West. It does describe, however, the view of the Islamist terrorists. If bin Ladin or someone of his ilk were to read Huntington's work [*The Clash of Civilizations and the Remaking of World Order*], the reaction would not be surprise or shock but rather acknowledgement that this indeed is the conflict in which they believe themselves engaged. In the terrorists' perception, it is a conflict that is based on religion, involves resistance to cultural intrusion, is inevitable, includes their own terrorist operations as a leading part, and in which the enemy is the West, whose core state is the United States of America.

Islam's Historical Grievances Against the West

The U.S. role as leader of the West entails a further reason for special resentment against it, beyond it being the source of the current cultural contamination that troubles the Islamists. The United States has inherited the baggage from centuries of conflict between the Islamic world and the West, going back to the Crusades and including the Christian re-conquest of Spain and later colonization by European pow-ers. Some of this history, despite its antiquity, remains promi-nent in many Muslim minds (including, but not only, the extremist ones), and underlies a sense that the Islamic world has been losing power at the hands of a hostile, relentless West. That the United States had responsibility for almost none of this history does not seem to absolve it from being its principal legatee. So for the Islamists, the contest is about not only a collision of cultures but also a need to restore lost power. To restore it, as [Israeli Middle East Scholar] Martin Kramer has written, "it must be subtracted from the Western powers, led by the United States, which dominate the Islamic world through instruments as diverse as movies, news net-works, banks, and cruise missiles." And for the terrorists, the symbolic value of striking the paramount Western power is at least as important as any details of either the history or the actual reasons for their current problems.

Misguided U.S. Policies in the Middle East Created the Problem of Islamic Terrorism

John Tirman

Writing shortly after the September 11 attacks, John Tirman argues that the attacks, and militant Islamic terrorism in general, are the result of U.S. actions in the Middle East. From supporting oppressive governments in Iran to arming Islamic fighters in Afghanistan, the United States played a large part in creating the problem of Islamic terrorism. Moreover, seeking to confront terrorism militarily, the United States will further incite militant Islamic sentiment. John Tirman is program director at the Social Science Research Council and author of *Spoils of War: The Human Cost of America's Arms Trade*.

All wars have unintended consequences. No matter how cautious generals and political leaders are, war sets in motion waves of change that can alter the currents of history. More often, generals and political leaders are not troubled by long-term side effects; they are sharply focused on achieving a victory and war's aims. The result is that the unseen and unintended occur, at times as a bitter riptide which overwhelms the original rationales for engaging in armed combat.

This unpredictable cycle of action and reaction has thwarted U.S. policy in southwestern Asia for 50 years. It began with attempts to contain the Soviet Union and control the oil-rich fields of the Persian Gulf, and continues today in the popular assault in Afghanistan to destroy the al-Qa'ida terrorist network. In that half century, nearly every major initiative led to an unexpected and sometimes cata-

John Tirman, "Unintended Consequences," www.alternet.org, October 24, 2001.

strophic reaction, for which new military remedies were devised, only again to stir unforeseen problems. The cycle, regrettably, may be repeating again.

U.S. Policy Toward Iran

The half-century history begins with CIA intrigue in Iran. The original spigot of Middle Eastern oil, Iran was long dominated by Britain and its oil company, British Petroleum. During World War II, strongman Reza Kahn, a Nazi sympathizer, was deposed by the British in favor of his son, Reza Shah, who in turn was shunted aside by the increasingly assertive parliament, the Majlis. In 1951, the Majlis elected as premier Mohammed Mossedegh, a nationalist reformer, who quickly sought control over Iran's oil wealth. The British, aghast at seeing 50 percent of British Petroleum's stake in Iran nationalized, sought his ouster, which the CIA provided in 1953. The Shah was reinstated and ruled with an iron fist, enabled by lavish American military aid.

The overthrow of Mossedegh remains a bitter memory for Iranians, and for Muslims more widely. While he was mainly a secular nationalist, even Islamic militants bewail his fate as another instance of Western interference and violence. In the years of the Shah's rule, many of the beleaguered reformers gravitated toward the *ulama*, the clerical class, who were relatively independent of the regime. So U.S. policy, which targeted the left as possible Soviet sympathizers or threats to oil interests, had the unintended effect of strengthening the political power and sophistication of the *ulama*.

By the 1970s, the Shah had become a self-styled regional power, flush with an unfettered flow of weaponry from the United States. Presidents Eisenhower and Kennedy, neither a wallflower when it came to arming allies against perceived Soviet expansionism, had bluntly dismissed the Shah's pleas for military supremacy, but President Nixon embraced the Shah without restraint. Not only were the newest jet fighters and other advanced weaponry made available, but endless commercial ties were created, bringing thousands of Americans to Teheran [capital of Iran]. In 1971, the Shah's oil minister launched a cascade of price increases that rocked the American economy for nearly a decade, but it was American guns and products that the ever-richer Shah and his cohort really sought. A widely perceived decadence eroded whatever support the regime maintained, and by the late 1970s, the Shah was struggling against the now-familiar Muslim "street" that detested the Westernized elite and resented their fabulous oil riches in the midst of poverty. In 1979, the Shah abdicated and left Iran in a stew of disarray. It was only a matter of months before the Islamic Revolution came to full flower.

The Devastating Aftermath

Apart from the war in Vietnam, where millions died, the U.S. role in imposing and sustaining the Shah in Iran is perhaps the most invidious episode in America's foreign policy. The consequences are colossal, and malignancies continue to appear. Among the first of these was the change in Soviet policy toward the region, and specifically in Afghanistan.

The Soviets had meddled in Afghanistan for years, supporting its on-again, off-again communist party. A mildly pro-Soviet regime in Kabul was under intense pressure from Islamic radicals in the late 1970s, however, and Moscow kept a wary eye on the chaotic events in neighboring Iran. As Islamic militancy gained in the post-Shah governments in Teheran, the Kabul regime became less and less tenable. In the Kremlin, the Soviet leadership opposed intervention until the Afghan regime was in complete turmoil. A high-level Russian, Georgy Kornienko, notes it was Defense Minister D.F. Ustinov who finally convinced the others to intervene:

> "The push to change his former point of view," he recalls in a memoir, "came from the stationing of American military ships in the Persian Gulf in the fall of 1979, and the incoming information about preparations for a possible American invasion of Iran, which threatened to cardinally change the military-strategic situation in the region to the detriment of the interests of the Soviet Union. If the United States can allow itself such things tens of thousands of kilometers away from their territory in the immediate proximity from the

USSR borders, why then should we be afraid to defend our positions in the neighboring Afghanistan?—this was approximately Ustinov's reasoning."

Politburo minutes from the entire previous year, now available, make clear the Soviet leaders' view that the Islamic militants were responsible for major attacks on government forces in Herat and elsewhere, and posed a threat, particularly with the active aid of the new [Ayatollah Ruhollah] Khomeini regime in Iran. The USSR, after all, included five Central Asia republics that were predominantly Muslim and bordered both Afghanistan and Iran. So the Shah's decades-long brutality gave rise to a broad Islamic movement in the region that, once in power in Teheran, not only alarmed Washington but also worried the much nearer Moscow.

The U.S. response to the collapse of the Shah, the triumph of Khomeini, and the December 1979 Soviet invasion of Afghanistan was to be played out tragically over the coming dozen years. Beginning with the Carter administration in the summer of 1979—months before the Soviets invaded—the CIA provided arms and training to the Afghan opposition, the now infamous *mujaheddin*, first to provoke the Soviets to ill-considered action (as Carter advisor Zbigniew Brzezinski has since revealed), and, after the December 1979 invasion, to make the Soviet stay in Afghanistan as inhospitable as possible. The large flow of arms and high-tech weapons like shoulder-launched anti-aircraft missiles did not come until 1986, by which time the Soviet leadership was firmly committed to departure. But a steady supply of Chinese-made AK-47s and Soviet-made weapons sent via Egypt provided the Islamic rebels with ample firepower to cripple the Soviets' aims in Afghanistan. It was, at the time, heralded as the wondrous victory of the "Reagan Doctrine," the strategy to arm "freedom fighters" against Soviet-leaning regimes in places like Angola and Nicaragua.

In all its venues and applications, the Reagan Doctrine had no qualms about the human costs of fomenting warfare, and most important for the present predicament, had no post-conflict strategy. The wages of war were high for all. Angola is still in a civil war more than 20 years later, with the

Reagan-backed Savimbi fueling a self-aggrandizing conflict. Nicaragua is devastated, impoverished; the Contras, who battled the Sandinista regime, engaged in a drug trade that now swamps the region.

So, too, with Afghanistan: the Soviets left in 1989, defeated, but their departure also left Afghanistan a political minefield (to go along with the 10 million real land mines left by both sides in the war). Warlords battled with each other for nearly a decade until the most extreme faction, the Taliban, gained ascendency in the late 1990s and provided the home to the terrorists the United States now seeks to rout. In the meantime, the 3 million AK-47s sent to the *mujaheddin* have been located as far away as Liberia and Mozambique, the fodder for other wars and misery. Professor Fred Halliday of the London School of Economics wrote at the end of the 1980s:

> The most striking feature of the Reagan Doctrine was the way in which Washington itself came to be a promoter and organizer of terrorist actions. The *mujaheddin* in Afghanistan, UNITA [a group fighting the Marxist government] in Angola and the Nicaraguan Contras were all responsible for abominable actions in their pursuit of "freedom"—massacring civilians, torturing and raping captives, destroying schools, hospitals and economic installations, killing and mutilating prisoners. . . . Reagan was responsible for the deaths of tens of thousands of people through terrorism.

Tilting Toward Iraq

At about the same time the Afghan resistance was being organized with U.S. aid, the Iraq regime of Saddam Hussein launched an attack on Iran to gain the oil fields on the gulf. This unprovoked act of war followed a period of quiet rapprochement with Washington (Brzezinski again), and throughout the ensuing eight years of carnage—in which one million people died—the U.S. government increasingly helped Iraq, supplying it with more than $5 billion in financial credits, intelligence data, heavy equipment like trucks and political respectability. In most estimates, the

U.S. "tilt" toward Baghdad was indispensable in saving Saddam from defeat.

The reason for the "tilt" was to frustrate the Islamic radicals in Teheran. This counter-Khomeini strategy extended beyond Iraq to countries like Turkey (where the U.S. approved a military coup in 1980 and suppression of Kurds, resulting in a civil war that has taken 30,000 lives) and Saudi Arabia (the keystone of U.S. oil policy, which led the U.S. to cast a blind eye on Saudi corruption and human-rights abuses). But Iraq, during the 1980s, was the centerpiece of this gambit.

After the catastrophic war of 1980–88, the new president, George Bush, embraced a policy of accommodation with Iraq. Within a few months of taking office, National Security Directive (NSD) 26 set the policy: "Access to Persian Gulf oil and the security of key friendly states in the area" were the two rationales of a strategy that would "pursue, and seek to facilitate, opportunities for U.S. firms to participate in the reconstruction of the Iraqi economy. . . . Also, as a means of developing access and influence with the Iraqi defense establishment, the United States should consider sales of non-lethal forms of military assistance." Said a senior official of NSD 26: "The concern over Iranian fundamentalism was a given." The Reagan-Bush accommodationist policy toward Iraq meant that Saddam received only a slap on the wrist for the murder, with chemical weapons, of 5,000 Kurds in the north at the end of the war with Iran.

But when Iraq occupied Kuwait in August 1990, the tilt fell over. The anti-Iran strategy, itself a response to the ruinous policy of supporting the Shah, now had unavoidable consequences: the long and devastating war in Afghanistan; intensified bloodshed in the Iran-Iraq war; the Kurdish massacres in Turkey and Iraq; an acceleration of Islamic militancy in Pakistan and civil war in Kashmir; and the subjugation of Kuwait and the threat to oil fields of Saudi Arabia. It has had other corollary effects, such as a tolerance of Syrian misdeeds, as well as devotion to the perversely corrupt and fragile House of Saud. . . . One must ask, in the wake of such an astounding set of catastrophes, if leaving Khomeini's Iran alone after 1980 would not have been less devastating in human terms, or whether Soviet "hegemony" over Afghanistan would not have been far better for Afghans, than 20 years of war, displacement and impoverishment.

The Next Catastrophe?

What will be next in this series of haunting mistakes? If this 50-year history teaches us anything, it is that aggressive military actions surely will earn a violent reaction, and that the pattern consistently displays three characteristics: large-scale human misery; the "involvement" of neighboring countries; and the amplification of militant Islamic sentiment around the world. In just a matter of weeks, all characteristics are now visible in the "war on terrorism.". . .

In the idiom of international relations, the most worrisome consequence is the perilous state of Pakistan. Coerced to cooperate with the United States, the military government is risking a revolt from below. Tensions with India are escalating over terrorist attacks in Kashmir [a disputed territory on the border between India and Pakistan], orchestrated perhaps by the same Pakistani military establishment we are now utilizing to attack Afghanistan. The worries about collapse or gradual disintegration of secular rule in Pakistan are punctuated by its possession of nuclear weapons. It is conceivable that within a few years the same sort of criminals who attacked the World Trade Center on Sept. 11 will have weapons of considerably greater power than four commercial jets. If one is comforted by the denigration of such scenarios by American officials, recall that they are the same group that engineered the accommodationist policy toward Iraq and the embrace of the *mujaheddin*. The eventual takeover of Islamabad by politically noxious "Islamicists" is a near certainty, if the war escalates or is prolonged, or if an equally dangerous clique gains control in Kabul. It is difficult to see how Pakistan can readily stabilize. . . .

The refugee flows and the anti-American sentiment among even moderate Muslims in the region also may destabilize Iran. The advances of moderation via civil society and the two electoral victories of President [Mohammed] Khatemi could be reversed as a result of the war in Afghanistan and the

American right wing's demands to antagonize Teheran as a "sponsor" of terrorism, along with the Taliban and Saddam. Internal political struggles in Iran were slowly being won by the forces of civility and democracy, but the "war on terrorism" may soon claim them as victims.

The calls to mount a campaign against Saddam, which is supported by Deputy Defense Secretary Paul Wolfowitz and the pundits at the *Washington Post*, is nearly beyond the pale of predictability if the administration is foolish enough to try it. Such a move, which would require a colossal military effort, would stir the Muslim street to threaten not only Pakistan and Iran, but Saudi Arabia and possibly other countries. These episodes of unrest in the region always reveal the decrepit state of the Saudi royal family, its immense debt from high living and corruption and the devil's bargain the U.S. has struck to preserve control of oil. There have been sizable, bloody riots even as far away as Nigeria and Indonesia.

The "war on terrorism," now conducted mainly on Afghan soil, is enough to stir these anti-American sentiments, although perhaps a short and precise military campaign is necessary and we will simply have to cope with the fallout. But a long bombing campaign, a lengthy American search-and-destroy mission in the Afghan countryside, a bloody assault on the Taliban and siege of Kabul—these unwarranted tactics, coupled with a refugee crisis, could inflame the tinderbox of Muslim sentiments. Invading Iraq would then only confirm their worst suspicions, that is, that Washington is intent upon destroying not just terrorists, but regimes in Muslim societies.

Steps Toward a Different Strategy

The goal of neutralizing or eliminating bin Laden and the al-Qa'ida network is laudable. Critics of American foreign policy should not mistake this network for folk heroes along the lines of Che Guevara or Franz Fanon. Al-Qa'ida is promoting a different order altogether, one that is violent at its core, not only in its complete rejection of pluralism and openness in Muslim societies, but in its repression of women and others. It is a dangerous and reactionary ideology in all respects. Christopher Hitchens has labeled it a form of fascism, which is not historically accurate, but the emotional meaning is resonant.

So how should the United States and its European allies deal with this danger? A detailed strategy is not something most of us are prepared to put forward, but some criteria are comprehensible. The first is to see this form of terrorism as acts of criminals rather than acts of warriors. ([Commentator] Hendrick Hertzberg in the *New Yorker* made this useful contrast right after the Sept. 11 attacks, saying that it ennobles the hijackers to call this a war; they are criminals.) Law enforcement, enhanced by the full throttle of intelligence services—including cooperation with allies—is the most likely way to foil al-Qa'ida over the long haul.

Aggressive investigations, detainment of plausible suspects, freezing financial assets and the like keep terrorists on the move, harassed and disrupted. Counter-communications strategies and pressure on thugs like the Saudi princes who fund al-Qa'ida will further immobilize them. This does mean a very long effort, stretching out over years; it is, in fact, one that has already been underway for years, but devalued and made inept by successive American presidents. A "law enforcement plus" strategy does involve some diplomatic resources and military actions that go beyond, for example, the longtime struggle against the mafia. One should not underestimate the disruptive power of killing bin Laden, if it can be quickly administered. But the longer term strategy is essentially one of old-fashioned techniques that require constant vigilance, cooperation across many borders and respect for law and its institutions, including an international criminal court, to bring the terrorists to justice.

America Must Become Independent of Mideast Oil

At the same time, coping with underlying causes of this terrorism and American vulnerabilities must be a priority. Here the Bush administration is especially weak or dissembling. The control of oil remains the linchpin of U.S. security policy in the region, and, indeed, the immediate reason for bin

Laden's rage is the stationing of U.S. troops in Saudi Arabia since Desert Shield [an international operation designed to protect Kuwait from Iraq] began in August 1990. American officials and opinion elites insist that we are there to protect our "access" to oil, but everyone in the world has access to oil; it's *control* over oil, and particularly the pricing of oil, which are at stake. There has been no energy policy for years, and the Bush energy proposals are not addressing the problem of gulf oil dependency at all. In part this is because American companies that do business there are close to the Bush administration (Halliburton, Dick Cheney's last employer, is one such firm), but it is also because to devise and implement an effective national strategy to reduce dependency on oil would require an enormous leap in fuel efficiency standards, a BTU [a unit of energy consumption] tax, and a sharp increase in use of conservation and other fuels (possibly including nuclear energy). These measures have been so devalued by conventional wisdom and resisted by pampered consumers they are simply unpalatable. Sacrifices may go as far as one-hour waits at airport security lines, but not to using a 75-mile-per-gallon small car or paying for big improvements in mass transit.

The problem of Muslim "rage" and the like is far more complex, of course, but certainly there are steps that can be taken. It is commonplace nowadays to hear that we don't explain ourselves well to the Muslim world, that we are represented mainly by MTV and "Melrose Place" (occasionally it's also acknowledged that it was a bad idea to decimate the foreign service and the U.S. Information Agency). While this view has some merit, it misses a much larger point: it's not just that we must tell our story better, we must *begin* to listen to what the concerns of the Muslim world actually are. This doesn't mean tuning in to the cacophony of the "street"; an enormous number of Western-oriented Muslim intellectuals are disenchanted with U.S. policies and can eloquently articulate the various critiques. That they have little sympathy for the U.S., despite Sept. 11, and see only further alienation as a result of the military assaults on Afghanistan, is alarming. In the broad U.S. political culture, we are not listening to such critiques, which is what is often meant by American arrogance: what we have to tell others is more important than what others have to tell us.

These kinds of approaches to the politics and security challenges of southwestern Asia and north Africa are just that—steps in what should be a much richer and complex national debate. That so many in the political and opinion establishment have resisted and even denounced such notions is a distressing sign of how uphill such steps will be. If we do care to absorb the lessons of the last 50 years in that region, however, we can do so only by engaging the history of policy failures (which beset all great powers) as well as the glory of the American dream. So much of that history is one of tragic and even catastrophic consequences, most of them unforeseen and unintended. We need now—immediately—to consider and act on those lessons both to honor the dead of Sept. 11 and to prevent more tragedy in the future.

Chapter 2

Debating the War on Terrorism

The War on Terror Is a Revolutionary Struggle

Michael Ledeen

In the following excerpt, Michael Ledeen challenges the conventional wisdom to declare that the war on terrorism is not a new type of war; rather, it is a revolutionary struggle similar to the U.S. War for Independence. Ledeen believes that the United States should embrace democratic opposition groups throughout the Islamic world. Policy makers need to overcome their fear of instability in the Middle East and support the expansion of democracy and civil rights throughout the region. With U.S. support, indigenous movements can overcome the authoritarian regimes in the area and establish true democratic governments. Ledeen is a fellow at the American Enterprise Institute, a conservative public policy research organization, and the author of several books and articles on various public policy issues.

The conventional mantra is that today's war on terrorism is a new kind of war, unlike those we have fought in the past. But that's not true.

We are currently waging a very old kind of war, and, as luck would have it, one that fits our national character and our unique military and political genius to a T. This is a revolutionary war, right out of the eighteenth century. While we will have to act quickly and urgently against secret terrorist organizations and suicidal fighters, our ultimate targets are tyrannical governments, and our most devastating weapons are the peoples they oppress.

In the Second World War, we defeated Japanese kamikazes

Michael Ledeen, "We'll Win This War," *The American Enterprise*, vol. 12, December 2001, pp. 22–25. Copyright © 2001 by The American Enterprise. Reproduced by permission.

in two ways: by fending them off more effectively, and by destroying the Tokyo regime. In like manner, we must both dismantle the terror network and destroy the regimes that have enabled them to become so threatening. Those who talk in abstract terms about various "stages" in this war, as if the two objectives were logically or strategically distinct, miss the point. We cannot destroy the terror network without bringing down the regimes, just as we could not end the siege of kamikaze terror without bringing down [Hideki] Tojo and his murderous state.

We have almost all the necessary weapons at hand, from our brilliant technological network of eyes in the sky and ears embedded in the world's telecom networks, to smart weapons and high-radiation devices and stealth aircraft. We have excellent Special Forces who can operate under the most difficult conditions and respond to rapidly changing circumstances. Don't believe the stories about our inability to operate in an Afghan winter. This is not the Light Brigade.

The United States: A Revolutionary Force

Even more important—and this is a weapon that is greatly underestimated by many of our intellectuals and diplomats—we are an awesome revolutionary force. Creative destruction is our middle name. We tear down the old order every day, in business and science, literature, art and cinema, politics and the law. Our present enemies hate this whirlwind of energy and creativity, which menaces their traditions and shames them for their inability to keep pace. Seeing America undo old conventions, they fear us, for they do not wish to be undone. They cannot feel secure so long as we are there, for our very existence—not our policies—threatens their legitimacy. They must attack us in order to survive, just as we must destroy them to advance our historic mission.

Behind all the anti-American venom from the secular radicals in Baghdad, the religious fanatics in Tehran, the minority regime in Damascus, and the kleptomaniacs in the Palestinian Authority, is the knowledge that they are hated by their own people. How could it be otherwise? Their power rests on terror directed against their citizens.

Given the chance to express themselves freely, the Iraqi, Iranian, Syrian, and Palestinian people would overturn their current oppressors. Properly waged, our revolutionary war will give them a chance to achieve exactly this. You need only listen to the screams of the Middle Eastern tyrants to realize that they fully understand the import of the struggle.

There is every reason to believe we will succeed in revolutionizing the Middle East, for we have always excelled at destroying tyrannies. The great democratic uprising at the end of the eighteenth century bore a clear American hallmark, and the entire twentieth century stands as tribute to the enormous power of our history—changing energies. Again and again we were dragged into war, and we invariably tossed our enemies onto history's trash heap of failed lies. We wage total war, because we fight in the name of an idea—freedom—and ideas either triumph or fail. Ask Mikhail Gorbachev.

We even overthrow tyrants when it is not our official aim. In the 1980s, President Reagan instructed the CIA to organize some Nicaraguans to disrupt the flow of weapons from Nicaragua to the Communist guerillas in El Salvador. The operation envisaged at most a few hundred people. But once American officials went into the field to recruit, thousands of anti-Communists, assuming this was the beginning of the end for the Sandinista regime in Nicaragua, raced to volunteer. They ultimately forced the Sandinistas to fight for their survival, and in time the regime fell.

The Task

George W. Bush has understood the scope of our task from the first minute, and I have no doubt that the assault on the Taliban tyranny in Afghanistan, and on the other terrorist regimes in the region, will be total. This is not a manhunt, it is the opening salvo of a great revolutionary war that will transform the Middle East. The president has started well, combining the destruction of Taliban infrastructure with near-simultaneous air drops of food and medicine to the tens of thousands of suffering refugees. Our message couldn't be clearer: We offer succor to the suffering Afghan people, and death to their evil leaders. That's what revolutionary warfare is all about—encouraging a popular insurrection, then supporting it.

We do not have all the weapons, however. Revolution requires revolutionary leaders, and some of these are lacking. There seem to be at least the elements of a transitional regime in Afghanistan, including the Northern Alliance [the alliance that fought against the Taliban government], some other anti-Taliban forces, and the long-suffering king [Mohammed Zahir Shah, exiled king of Afghanistan] waiting his call in Rome. I am one of those who thought we should have supported [Ahmad Shah] Massoud, the charismatic Northern Alliance leader who was assassinated by a suicide killer just two days before September 11, because he was the only one of the fighters who seemed to me to have the requisite leadership qualities. Lacking that kind of leader, the next Afghan government is likely to be transient.

There is no reason for us to be overly worried about that, though. Yes, I know that our diplomats hate "instability," but most Americans are not only able to cope with it, they go out of their way to create it. Stability is for those older, burnt-out countries, not for the American dynamo. And chaos is vastly preferable to the vicious tyrannical stability that has crushed and impoverished the people of Afghanistan.

U.S. Policy Toward Iraq

In Iraq, we have long pretended to support the Iraqi National Congress and its leader Ahmed Chalabi, a man at once democratic and tough-minded, whose family has played a major role in regional politics for nearly 500 years. The Clinton administration gave the INC some money and CIA advice, and promised to defend them if Saddam moved against their haven in the north. They did well enough to provoke Saddam into a risky throw of the dice: In the mid 1990s he sent the bulk of his tanks into the north, exposing them to our airpower. Clinton had plenty of advance warning, sufficient for the National Security Council to reiterate our promise to defend Chalabi, and he warned Saddam of a harsh response if Iraq invaded the north.

But at the moment of truth the Clinton administration

abandoned our friends; the INC was massacred, and the survivors went into exile. The bad news is that we betrayed good allies. The good news is that a remnant of the INC force lived to fight again another day. And Saddam's risky strike against them shows that he takes their threat seriously.

Congress took up the cudgels and, toward the end of the Clinton years, appropriated money for the Iraqi resistance. One might have expected the new Bush administration to vigorously support this, but the State Department fought tooth and nail against commitments to the Iraqi National Congress, dribbling out a tiny fraction of the appropriated funds, and then only for administrative expenses and the production of a bit of propaganda. Moreover, our diplomats warned Chalabi against spending one penny for in-country activities. Those restrictions must be immediately removed; the Iraqi people need to see there is a real alternative, on the ground, to Saddam's grotesque regime.

Can a group like the INC, given American assistance, catalyze a successful insurrection against a murderous regime? This is the key question for our policy makers, and it applies to all the terrorist states. The answer is, we don't know. But our experiences in Central America in the 1980s give reason for optimism. The lesson from Nicaragua is that the world changes quickly once people see that the United States is seriously engaged.

In Iraq, the spontaneous uprisings of diverse portions of the population at the end of the Gulf War—from the Kurds in the north to the Shiites in the south—are evidence that the oppressed people of that country would love to destroy Saddam's regime. There are similar indications elsewhere in the region.

Popular Support for Revolution

In Iran, there are many brave people who have risked, and often lost, their lives to challenge the mullahcracy, ranging from the outspoken students at Tehran University to the more cautious reformers who have taken shelter under the robes of President [Mohammed] Khatami. We broadcast words of hope to the Iranian people from freedom-minded exiles through our Radio Freedom satellite, which greatly disturbs the ayatollahs. But this is not nearly enough. We must announce our support for Iranian democrats, and our unrelenting rejection of the theocracy that has, at least as much as any other, provided the wherewithal for international terrorism.

In Syria, too, there is every reason to expect great public support for a campaign to remove the Assad regime. Here again the evidence comes from the most reliable source: the regime itself. Some years ago, [Syrian president] Hafez al Assad crushed dissent in the city of Hama, killing as many as 20,000 people, then bulldozing the evidence into the dirt. Any regime compelled to assert its legitimacy in such a violent manner is profoundly insecure, and that insecurity is invariably based on hard knowledge of popular discontent.

In Sudan, a nasty civil war has been raging for years, and our slowly increasing pressure on the Islamic regime in Khartoum—which has been killing the southern Christians and animists seems to be working. It may be possible to impose an end to the north's military campaign, demand active cooperation in intelligence sharing, terminate Sudanese support for terrorist groups (and the surrender of any terrorists), and permit the creation of an independent state in the south, in exchange for a guarantee that we will not do to Sudan what we have done to Afghanistan.

If we had a CIA worthy of the name we would know more about the brave people in Iran and Iraq, as well as in Syria and Sudan, and of course the Palestinians who groan under Arafat's corrupt tyranny. All realize they can live better, and we should be supporting them in that quest. Alas, we are reluctant nation-builders. We had no alternative to Saddam during the Gulf War, just as we were unprepared for the political battles that followed the fall of Nazism, the Japanese warlords, and the Soviet Empire.

This time there is no excuse. There are people ready to fight for our common objectives behind enemy lines, if only we get to work. We must wage revolutionary war against all the terrorist regimes, and gradually replace them with governments that turn to their own people's freely expressed desires as the basis of their political legitimacy.

The Problem of Saudi Arabia

That leaves Saudi Arabia. Back in the 1970s, at the time of the fall of the Shah of Iran, our Middle East strategy was said to rest on two pillars: Iranian military power, and Saudi money. The Shah fell for two reasons. First, he lacked the will to fight for his own survival when challenged by religious fanatics. Second, he got caught in the transition between traditional society and a more modern one: Iran was insufficiently liberal to fulfill the desires of the westernizing middle class, and insufficiently hard-line to satisfy those who feared modernization. So the Shah pleased no one.

I have long argued that the United States is obliged to work with friendly dictators to achieve successful transitions to societies more in keeping with American values. We should insist on steady liberalization at the same time we provide full support to the friendly tyrants if they are challenged by forces that will make things even worse. Saudi Arabia offers us a great second chance to succeed in the region after our failure with the Shah. There is certainly a Westernizing middle class beneath the arch-reactionary veneer of the Wahabi [an ultra-strict sect of Islam] tyrants who have been the primary source of funding and religious proselytizing for Islamic extremists in the Middle East. We should offer the Saudi ruling elite our support for their survival—provided they become a moderate Islamic regime in practice, not just words.

Saudi Arabia is the most difficult challenge, and the most important, and for those reasons it is the policy crisis that our diplomats most often decline to address. But if we pursue revolutionary war against terrorist regimes, our ability to influence events in Saudi Arabia will greatly increase. If we understand our mission rightly, we will find myriad opportunities to help the Saudis move in productive directions.

We have a glorious opportunity to improve life on our planet, and we are the right people, at the right time, to pull it off. The most dangerous threat to our success is limited vision and insufficient ambition. If we act like the revolutionary force we truly are, we can once again reshape the world, as we repeatedly did throughout the last century. But if we settle for token victories and limited accomplishments, we will permit our enemies to reorganize, and attack us with even greater venom in the future.

We do not want a replay of the Gulf War. This time we must fight for keeps.

America Should Not Respond to Terrorism with Military Force

The *Progressive*

The *Progressive* is a long-established, left-wing magazine. In this editorial written immediately after the attacks of September 11, the editors of the magazine warn against a war of revenge. The editors make three main points in their argument: Congress must declare a war for the action to be constitutional, U.S. actions have provoked the terror attacks, and civil liberties will be in danger during the war on terror. The public must not get swept up by a desire for revenge, only to abandon constitutional rights. Nor can the United States think of itself as blameless. Rather, the United States must reexamine its foreign policy in order to determine what might have caused these attacks.

We write just one day after the terrible terrorist attack on New York City and the Pentagon. We are in shock, as is the rest of the nation. We grieve for the thousands who died, the thousands who are wounded, and their families.

But we resist the call to arms, and we are made sick by the blood lust in the media and among the populace.

The United States should protect itself and its citizens—no doubt. That is a constitutional requirement, and the obligation of all nation states. But to wage war may only seed the clouds for future acts of terror. And to act precipitously, as it seems [President] George W. Bush will do, all but guarantees that the United States will hit some wrong targets and inflict needless suffering on hundreds—maybe thousands—of innocent people.

Recall the Clinton bombing of the Sudanese pharmaceu-

The Progressive, "The Toll of Terror," vol. 65, October 2001, pp. 8–11. Copyright © 2001 by The Progressive, Inc. Reproduced by permission.

tical plant in Khartoum in 1998, which destroyed much of the medical supplies for that country. Clinton said the plant was linked to nerve gas production, but never produced the evidence. Recall the missiles during that same bombing mission that strayed into Pakistan instead of hitting their targets in Afghanistan. Are we going to see more of those?

Bush seems indifferent to the "collateral damage" that any large military action will cause. But what kind of morality is it for Bush to decry the killing of civilians and then go out and kill some civilians himself?

Only Congress Has the Right to Declare War

Commentators tell us that this is the second Pearl Harbor. On December 8, 1941, FDR got a declaration of war from Congress. No Congress has issued such a declaration since, though President after President has waged war. If Bush is to go to war, the least he could do is follow the requirements of Article 1, Section 8, of our Constitution. Otherwise, it will be another lawless act, and another diminution of our democracy.

The Pearl Harbor analogy has frightening connotations. Two months after Japan's surprise attack, the U.S. government rounded up Japanese Americans into internment camps. Now it seems highly improbable that Arab Americans or Muslim Americans will be rounded up, but what does seem quite possible is that the media's obsessive focus on a non-differentiated Islamic fundamentalism—mixed in with nativist sentiment that is always on the shelf—will create a cocktail of hate crimes.

"We should drop nuclear weapons on all of Islam," said one anonymous caller, who left a message with American Muslims for Global Peace and Justice in Santa Clara, California.

"Islamic Americans in many cities have already been grappling with an angry backlash," The Wall Street Journal reported on September 12. "Salam School, an Islamic elementary school in Milwaukee, evacuated its 372 students after receiving two threatening phone calls. Meanwhile, Islamic schools in Southern California were evacuated, [and] a Fort Worth, Texas, mosque received a bomb threat."

The Council on American-Islamic Relations, based in Washington, D.C., recommended several security precautions be taken. "Those who wear Islamic attire should consider staying out of public areas for the immediate future," was one such precaution.

Civil Liberties Threatened

Meanwhile, the civil liberties of all Americans are under threat. ABC News conducted a poll on the evening of September 11 that showed 66 percent of Americans were in favor of curtailing civil liberties if it made them more secure. And officials were quick to go on the air with proposals that domestic surveillance be increased.

Civil liberties, like truth, are a casualty of war. It is not something we should roll over for.

In his primetime speech to the nation on September 11, President Bush said, "America was targeted for attack because we're the brightest beacon for freedom and opportunity in the world."

Not knowing with any certainty who the attackers were, it's hard to speculate on their motives. But many groups in the Third World have grievances that are more specific than the ones Bush mentioned, such as U.S. support for the corrupt Saudi regime, or Israel's ongoing occupation of Palestinian land and its suppression of the intifada.

No grievance, however, justifies the killing of innocent people. No grievance can make the acts of September 11, anything less than the ghoulish, heartless attack that they were. Those behind the acts should be apprehended and prosecuted to the full extent of the law.

But we do need to examine the roots of terrorism. And the United States has wittingly and unwittingly cultivated many of them.

In the case of Osama Bin Laden, Washington's chief suspect, it needs to be recalled that he was a creature of the CIA. In the 1980s, the United States put out an all-points-bulletin for Islamic fundamentalists to come to Afghanistan to fight the Soviet Union. Bin Laden was among them. "He is said to have received considerable money during the ten-year

Afghan battle from the U.S. Central Intelligence Agency," the Associated Press reported on September 12.

(Ironically, many officials and former officials are saying the United States needs to loosen up the laws that restrict the CIA from recruiting people with unsavory human-rights records. These officials say we need to increase our "human assets," but what does that mean: We're going to put more Bin Ladens on the payroll?)

Ahmed Rashid's latest book, *Taliban* (Yale University Press, 2000), quotes Bin Laden as saying that American officers helped him set up his first camp in Afghanistan. "The weapons were supplied by the Americans, the money by the Saudis," he says in the book.

Rashid gives the background: "Between 1982 and 1992, some 35,000 Muslim radicals from forty-three Islamic countries in the Middle East, North and East Africa, Central Asia, and the Far East would pass their baptism under fire with the Afghan Mujaheddin. Tens of thousands more foreign Muslim radicals came to study, along the Afghan border. Eventually, more than 100,000 Muslim radicals were to have direct contact with Pakistan and Afghanistan and be influenced by the jihad.

"In camps near Peshawar and in Afghanistan, these radicals met each other for the first time and studied, trained, and fought together. It was the first opportunity for most of them to learn about Islamic movements in other countries, and they forged tactical and ideological links that would serve them well in the future. The camps became virtual universities for future Islamic radicalism.

"None of the intelligence agencies involved wanted to consider the consequences of bringing together thousands of Islamic radicals from all over the world. 'What was more important in the worldview of history? The Taliban or the fall of the Soviet Empire? A few stirred-up Muslims or the liberation of Central Europe and the end of the Cold War?' said Zbigniew Brzezinski, a former U.S. National Security Adviser."

This boomerang effect is what intelligence officers call "blowback." And what is blowing back is a virulent strain of religious fundamentalism, and a large cadre of Muslim fanatics trained in modern warfare.

Bin Laden became further radicalized during the Gulf War [fought in 1991, the United States liberated Kuwait after that country had been occupied by Iraq]. He "openly accused Saudi Arabia's King Fahd of selling the holy sites of Islam to the United States," the A.P. noted.

With that, he was off and running, first to the Sudan, and then back to Afghanistan.

Other U.S. policies have also served, unwittingly, as recruiting calls for terrorists. The sanctions against Iraq (and the regular bombings that have occurred in the years since the Gulf War) have appalled much of the world. And unconditional U.S. support for Israel, its chief ally in the Middle East, has enraged the Muslim world. Israel's thirty-four-year occupation of Palestinian land and its ongoing repression of Palestinians during the second intifada have raised tensions not only in the Middle East but throughout the Arab and Muslim world.

These may be some of the contributing factors behind the targeting of America. Others include: global poverty, bigotries of all stripes, nationalism, and a religious fanaticism that says any means—no matter how gruesome—are justified in the service of the cause.

To note these factors is not, by any means, to justify the actions of the terrorists. It is only to suggest that the United States should be careful not to pursue policies that are unjust or needlessly inflammatory. The United States will not be able to preempt the ravings of every madman, but it can see to it that it does not send thousands of people into the arms of such madmen.

The calls for retribution came swiftly, and from all quarters. One poll showed more than 90 percent of the American people in favor of military action. Another said two-thirds were in favor even if it meant that innocent lives would be lost.

But what will an attack achieve?

Bush appears to be planning a huge military action, perhaps including the bombing and invasion of Afghanistan. Other targets may be on the boards. How many innocent people will die in this act of vengeance against the killing of innocent people?

War Will Sow Seeds of Future Terror

And how many seeds of terror will the U.S. retaliation sow?

We should remember that when President Reagan sent jets to bomb Muammar Qaddafi's tent in April 1986, a raid that killed one of Qaddafi's kids, it spurred its own act of revenge. A Libyan agent was convicted of the 1988 downing of Pan Am Flight 103 over Lockerbie, Scotland, which killed 270 people. Prosecutors said the agent was out to settle the score.

This cycle of violence must be broken. The time to break it is now.

One last point. George W. Bush said this is a conflict of "good versus evil." But the United States has a long way to go before it can put the halo of "good" over its head.

If the United States truly abhors the killing of innocent people, it must stop the killing of innocent people in Iraq with the weapon of economic sanctions.

If the United States truly abhors the killing of innocent people, it must throw its weight behind reaching a peace accord in Colombia [where a guerilla war has raged for decades] rather than funding the military there, which is complicit in thousands of human rights abuses.

If the United States truly abhors the killing of innocent people, it must intercede with Israel and insist on the return of the Occupied Territories to the Palestinian Authority.

A little humble reckoning is in order, too. "The policies of militarism pursued by the United States have resulted in millions of deaths," the War Resisters League noted on September 11. And that is, indeed, the grisly record: three million in Indochina, one million in Indonesia and East Timor, tens of thousands in Latin America, thousands more in Africa and the Middle East.

"Let us seek an end of the militarism that has character- ized this nation for decades," the staff and executive com- mittee of the War Resisters League said on September 11. "Let us seek a world in which security is gained through dis- armament, international cooperation, and social justice—

not through escalation and retaliation."

Those are wise words, and we would do well to heed them in this time of terror.

The easy response is the military one. That's what the people clamor for. That's what the media clamor for. That's what U.S. precedent would require. But it is not the moral or the sensible line of action.

To pile innocent body upon innocent body will do no one—and no nation—any good.

Opponents of the War on Terrorism Are Misguided

Mark Steyn

In the following selection, Mark Steyn criticizes activists and commentators who oppose military action in the war on terrorism. He argues that these opponents of the war resort to the use of meaningless clichés about the "root causes" of terrorism—such as poverty, despair, and U.S. policies—rather than holding the terrorists accountable for their actions. In their attempts to justify terrorism, Steyn contends, antiwar protesters minimize the horror of the harm inflicted on the innocent victims. Steyn is an author who specializes in politics, arts, and culture. In Canada, his writings appear in the *National Post*. In the United Kingdom, he is a columnist for the *Daily* and *Sunday Telegraph* and North American correspondent and film critic of the *Spectator*. In the United States, he appears in the *Chicago Sun-Times* and is also theater critic of the *New Criterion*.

What have we learnt since 11 September? We've learnt that poverty breeds despair, despair breeds instability, instability breeds resentment, and resentment breeds extremism.

Yes, folks, these are what we in the trade call 'root causes'. Which cause do you root for? 'Poverty breeds instability' (the *Detroit News*)? Or 'poverty breeds fanaticism' (Carolyn Lochhead in the *San Francisco Chronicle*)?

Bear in mind that 'instability breeds zealots' (John Ibbitson in the *Toronto Globe and Mail*), but that 'fanaticism breeds hatred' (Mauve MacCormack of New South Wales) and 'ha-

Mark Steyn, "People Who Hate People," *Spectator*, vol. 287, October 6, 2001, p. 24. Copyright © 2001 by The Spectator, Ltd. Reproduced by permission.

tred breeds extremism' (Mircea Geoana, Romanian Foreign Minister).

Above all, let's not forget that 'desperation breeds resentment' (Howard Zinn in the *Los Angeles Times*) and 'resentment breeds terrorism' (Eugene G. Wollaston of Naperville, Illinois), but sometimes 'desperation breeds terrorism' (a poster in Lower Manhattan) as surely as 'despair breeds terrorism' (Ian Lawson in the *San Diego Union-Tribune*), though occasionally 'despair breeds pestilence' (James Robertson of Ashland, Oregon).

Moreover, 'injustice breeds hopelessness' (Stephen Bachhuber of Portland, Oregon) and 'hopelessness breeds fanaticism' (Mark McCulloch of Forest Hills, Pennsylvania) and 'injustice breeds rage' (the National Council of Churches).

Also, 'ignorance breeds hate' (Wasima Alikhan of the Islamic Academy of Las Vegas), just as 'hostility breeds violence' (Alexa McDonough, leader of Canada's New Democratic Party), and 'suffering breeds violence' (David Pricco of San Francisco) and 'war breeds hate and hate breeds terrorism' (Julia Watts of Berkeley, California) and 'intolerance breeds hate, hate breeds violence and violence breeds death, destruction and heartache' (David Coleman of the University of Oklahoma).

'Injustice breeds injustice' (Dr L.B. Quesnel of Manchester) and 'suffering breeds suffering' (Gabor Mate, author of *Scattered Minds: A New Look at the Origins and Healing of Attention Deficit Disorder*) and 'instability breeds instability' (Congressman Alcee Hastings) and 'hate breeds hate' (a sign at the University of Maryland) and 'hatred breeds hatred' (the Reverend Charles A. Summers of the First Presbyterian Church of Richmond, Virginia) and 'anger breeds anger. Hostility breeds hostility. And attacks are going to breed other attacks' (Dania Dandashly of the Governor Bent Elementary School in Albuquerque, New Mexico), all of which only further confirms that—all together now—'violence breeds violence'. So say Bishop Thomas Gumbleton of Detroit, and Kathleen McQuillen of the American Friends Service Committee, and Chris Struble, President of Humanists of Idaho, and Riane Eisler, international activist for peace, human rights and the environment, macro-historian, systems and cultural-transformation theorist and President of the Center for Partnership Studies.

Generalities and Cliches

I hate to be 'partisan' about this, really I do. If there's one thing that's clear since 11 September, it's that the familiar identity-group labels aren't the ones that really define us. What matters about Mark Bingham, one of the brave men who overpowered the hijackers of Flight 93 and thus saved potentially thousands of lives, is not that he was gay or even that he was a Republican but that he was a great American hero. What matters about the Revd Jerry Falwell, who declared that the mass slaughter was God's judgment on gays, feminists et al., is not that he's a social conservative (as I am) but that he's a heartless jerk.

That said, a large swath of the Left has settled into an endless dopey roundelay, a vast Schnitzlerian carousel where every abstract noun is carrying on like Anthony Quinn on Viagra. Instability breeds resentment, resentment breeds inertia, inertia breeds generalities, generalities breed cliches, cliches breed lame metaphors, until we reach the pitiful state of the peacenik opinion columns where, to modify the old evening news motto, if it breeds it leads. If I were to say 'Mr Scroggins breeds racing pigeons', it would be reasonable to assume that I'd been round to the Scroggins house or at least made a phone call. But the 'injustice breeds anger' routine requires no such mooring to humdrum reality, though it's generally offered as a uniquely shrewd insight, reflecting a vastly superior understanding of the complexities of the situation than we nuke-crazy warmongers have. 'What you have to look at is the underlying reasons,' a Dartmouth College student said to me the other day. 'Poverty breeds resentment and resentment breeds anger.'

'Really?' I said. 'And what's the capital of Saudi Arabia?'

It's certainly possible to mount a trenchant demolition of US policy toward Israel, Palestine, Kuwait, Iraq, Iran, Afghanistan and Pakistan, but that would require specifics, facts, a curiosity about the subject, and this breed of rhetoric is designed to save you the trouble. It's certainly not worth rebutting: if poverty and despair breed terrorism, then how come AIDS-infested sub-Saharan Africa isn't a hotbed of terrorism? Needless to say, it's also racist, or more accurately culturalist: the non-Western world is apparently just one big petri dish full of mutating globules, eternally passive, acted upon but never acting. As Salman Rushdie wrote of 11 September, 'To excuse such an atrocity by blaming US government policies is to deny the basic idea of all morality: that individuals are responsible for their actions.' And the fact that only one side is denied this essential dignity of humanity tells you a lot about what the peace crowd really think of them.

But the breed screed is revealing of the broader disposition of its speakers. In America, the Right tend to be federalists, the Left centralists. The Right are happy to leave education to local school boards, the Left want big Federal government programmes. The Right say hire a new local police chief and let him fix the crime problem, the Left demand Federal hate-crimes legislation. The Right favour individual liberties, the Left are more concerned with group rights. In a nutshell, the Right are particular, the Left love generalities (if you'll forgive a generalisation).

Dehumanizing the Victims

And so faced with the enormity of 11 September the pacifist Left has done what it always does—smother the issues in generalities and abstractions—though never on such an epic scale. On that sunny Tuesday morning, at least 7,000 [the death toll from the attacks was subsequently revised to approximately 3,000] people died—real, living men and women and children with families and street addresses and telephone numbers. But the language of the pacifists—for all its ostensible compassion—dehumanises these individuals. They're no longer flight attendants and firemen and waitresses and bond dealers, but only an abstract blur in some theoretical equation—not yet 'collateral damage' (the phrase they loved to mock the militarists for), but certainly collateral. Of course, real live folks die in the Middle East, too, and their stories are worth telling. But in between the bone-

head refrains of this breeding that and that breeding the
other, you'll search in vain for a name or a face, a street or a
city or sometimes even a country. Just the confident asser-
tion that one abstract noun breeds another.

The totalitarian grotesqueness of the 'peace movement'
was nicely caught in the photos of [an October 2001] demonstration in Washington. The usual anti-globalisation crowd
had pencilled in the end of September for their protest against
the IMF and World Bank. The IMF and World Bank decided
to postpone their meeting, but the glob mob figured there was
no reason to call off the demo. So instead they got their
rewrite guys in and switched all the placards from anti-
capitalist slogans to anti-war slogans. This prompted a
counter-protest by locals who held up signs reading 'SHAME
FOR DISTURBING A CITY IN MOURNING'.

Just so. These people are mourning family, neighbours,
acquaintances. If you're going to intrude on that, you could
at least come up with something more pertinent than boiler-
plate sloganeering. It's true that with so many corpses—I use
the term loosely as most of the victims were atomised—it's
hard to focus on the individuals, the faces in the crowd. 'It
was the Hansons I fastened on,' Anna Quindlen wrote in
Newsweek. 'No telling why, exactly, except perhaps for the
way their names appeared on the flight list, with that single
number:

"Peter Hanson, Massachusetts "Susan Hanson, Massachusetts "Christine Hanson, 2, Massachusetts."

I've been critical of *Newsweek*'s back-of-the-book sob-
sister, but she puts it very well: our common humanity requires us 'to see ourselves in them all: the executives, the
waiters, the lawyers, the police officers, the father, the
mother, the 2-year-old girl off on an adventure, sitting safe
between them, taking wing.' At one brokerage firm alone—
Cantor Fitzgerald—there are 1,500 children who've lost one
of their parents. Picture a four-year-old girl on an otherwise
perfectly normal day wondering why mommy's crying and
why daddy isn't there to tuck her up in bed, and the next day
he's still not there, and the next, and then mommy tells you

he won't be coming home any more and that he's gone to heaven, which is nice for him, but you wish he would come back to read you one more story. And you get older and go to school and daddy fades into a blur, just a couple of indistinct memories of a face leaning over your pillow and you feel him only as an absence, a part of your childhood stolen from you. Multiply that by 1,500 for Cantor Fitzgerald and then throw in all the other orphans. I 'fastened on' Carol Flyzik, a lesbian nurse who'd got up early and headed for Logan airport in Boston from Plaistow, a town in southern New Hampshire I drive through from time to time. She lived with her partner and their children and, although I'm a notorious homophobe and no respecter of 'alternative families', I can't see what on earth those kids did to deserve having a great, gaping hole blown into their lives.

Acknowledging the Human Toll

Why do some people look at a smoking ruin and see the lives lost—the secretary standing by the photocopier—and others see only confirmation of their thesis on Kyoto? This isn't being sentimental. Any real insight into the 'root causes' has to begin with an acknowledgment of the human toll, if only because that speaks more eloquently than anything else to the vast cultural gulf between the victims and perpetrators. To deny them their humanity, to reduce them to an impersonal abstraction is Stalinist. Bill Clinton at least claimed to 'feel your pain'. The creepy, inhuman formulations of the peace movement can't even go through the motions.

Few of us would have bet on the professors, preachers and the rest of the educated, articulate Left performing in quite such a desultory, slap-dash fashion. But in bringing war to the East Coast for the first time in two centuries the terrorists have also brought the fellow travellers home. It was easy to slough off the dead in the gulags, far away and out of sight. But could they do the same if the dead were right here on this continent, and not in some obscure cornpone hicksville but in the heart of our biggest cities? Yes, they could, and so easily. At one level, it's simply bad taste—a lack of breeding, so to speak. But the interesting thing, to those of us used to being reviled as right-wing haters, is how sterile the vocabulary of those who profess to 'love' and 'care' is. In some weird Orwellian boomerang, the degradation of language required to advance the Left's agenda has rendered its proponents utterly desiccated. The President gets teary in the Oval Office, the Queen chokes up at St Paul's, David Letterman and Dan Rather sob on CBS, New Yorkers weep openly for their slain firemen, but the dead-eyed zombies of the peace movement who claim to love everyone parade through the streets unmoved, a breed apart.

Official Justifications for the War on Terror Are False

Rahul Mahajan

Rahul Mahajan is a graduate student in physics at the University of Texas at Austin and an antiwar activist serving on the National Boards of Peace Action and the Education for Peace in Iraq Center. His writings on foreign policy and globalization have been published in newspapers including the *Baltimore Sun* and *Houston Chronicle* and alternative publications such as *Extra!* and the *Texas Observer*.

In this sharp dissent from popular opinion, Mahajan refutes—point by point—the mainstream media's claims about the war on terrorism. The media have portrayed the Islamicists led by Osama bin Laden as being against freedom, but they are really against U.S. policy in the Middle East. According to Mahajan, the U.S. campaign in Afghanistan was not justified because the people of Afghanistan posed no threat to the United States. Moreover, the Afghan campaign was not conducted in a way that limited civilian casualties. Mahajan claims that U.S. citizens must examine their own government's crimes in order to understand the September 11 attacks.

The world changed on September 11. That's not just media hype. The way some historians refer to 1914–1991 as the "short twentieth century," many are now calling September 11, 2001, the real beginning of the twenty-first century. It's too early to know whether that assessment will be borne out, but it cannot simply be dismissed.

The attacks of September 11 forever ended the idea that the United States could somehow float above the rest of the

Rahul Mahajan, "The New Crusade: America's War on Terrorism," *Monthly Review*, vol. 53, February 2002, pp. 15–23. Copyright © 2002 by Monthly Review Press. Reproduced by permission.

earth, of it and not of it at the same time. Americans can no longer foster the illusion that what happens to the rest of the world doesn't affect them. It is more crucial than ever that we understand what kind of world we are living in, and what the United States has done to make it what it is.

It is not enough to say that the attacks were crimes against humanity, though they were, and that terrorism like that must be stopped, though it must. It's also not enough to say that the hijackers were religious extremists, though they were. One must also understand the role the United States has played in promoting religious extremism, directly, as in the Afghan jihad [holy war], and indirectly, by destroying all alternatives through its ceaseless attacks on the left and by pursuing policies that foster resentment and anger.

Refuting the Myths

It is of particular importance to understand its newest policies, the so-called "war on terrorism." Of the many ways to approach it, perhaps the most straightforward is to examine the official view of the war on terrorism that has emerged and is being pushed on the public, and refuting it point by point. These are some of the main myths about that war:

The attack was like Pearl Harbor, and therefore, as in the Second World War, we had to declare war or risk destruction. The truth is that Pearl Harbor was an attack by a powerful, expansionist state that had the capacity to subjugate all of East Asia. The attacks of September 11 were committed by nineteen men, part of a series of networks that has a few thousand hard-core militants, with access to modest financial resources. Since they were hardly an immediate, all-encompassing threat, options other than war could have been explored.

This was an attack on freedom. Whatever considerations exist in the mind of Osama bin Laden or members of his network, his recently broadcast statements contain no mention of any resentment of American democracy, freedom, or the role of women. They mention specific grievances regarding U.S. policy in the Middle East: the sanctions on Iraq, maintained largely by the United States, which have killed over one million civilians; material and political support for Israel's military occupation of Palestine and its frequent military attacks, carried out with American weapons, on practically unarmed Palestinians; and U.S. military occupation of the Gulf and support for corrupt regimes that serve the interests of U.S. corporations before those of the people. The terrorists' own vision for the states of the Middle East is, if imaginable, even more horrific than the current reality, and would presumably involve even greater limits on freedom than are already in place. Their recruiting points, however, the issues that make them potentially relevant as a political force, have to do with U.S. domination of the region, not with the internal organization of American society.

You're with us or you're with the terrorists. This polarization, foisted on the world to frighten possible dissenters from America's course of action, is the logic of tyranny, even of extermination. Anti-war protesters who condemn the terrorist attacks of September 11 along with the criminal acts of the United States in Afghanistan, and countries that do the same, don't fit into this scheme, and certainly don't deserve to be tarred with the same brush as the terrorists.

The war on Afghanistan was self-defense. In fact, people in Afghanistan at the time of the attack had no way of menacing the United States from afar since they have no ICBMs [intercontinental ballistic missiles] or long-range bombers. Someone in Afghanistan intending to attack the United States had to get there first. If there was an imminent threat, it was from terrorists already in the United States or in Europe. Thus, there was enough time to seek Security Council authorization, which is required unless one is attacking the source of an imminent threat. Instead, the U.S. deliberately chose not to seek it. The four weeks between the attack and the war that passed virtually without incident are proof that there was no immediate, overwhelming need for military action, a fundamental requirement of any claim to act in self-defense.

The Bush administration turned away from its emerging unilateralism (pulling out of the Kyoto protocols [an international treaty to control global warming], sabotaging the ABM [antiballistic missile] treaty with Russia, etc.) to a new multilateralism. This assumes that "multilateralism" means first predetermining one's agenda, then attempting to browbeat or bribe other countries into agreement or acquiescence. True multilateralism would involve setting up international structures that are democratic, transparent, and accountable to the people, institutions, and governments of the world and abiding by the decisions of these authorities whether favorable or not. The United States has consistently set itself against any such path. In this case, the United States refused even to seek the authority from the appropriate body in this case, the Security Council. This even though the United States could likely have gained its acquiescence by use of its standard methods of threats and bribery. It seems that the United States wishes very firmly and deliberately to claim the right of unilateral aggression.

There were four weeks of restraint as the Bush administration tried a diplomatic solution to the problem. Much of the "restraint" was simply to find time to move troops and materiel into place and to browbeat reluctant countries like Pakistan, Uzbekistan, and Tajikistan [both Central Asian countries bordering on Afghanistan] into providing staging areas and overflight rights. Also, there was real concern about destabilizing many allied governments in the Islamic world. No diplomatic solution was tried; the administration line was consistently "no negotiations." They made demands no sovereign country could accept; free access of the U.S. military to sensitive sites, plus the right arbitrarily to demand that an unspecified group of people be "turned over." They also refused to present the Taliban with evidence. In spite of all this, the Taliban was willing to negotiate delivery to a neutral third party. In fact, a deal had been worked out to have bin Laden tried in Pakistan by a tribunal which would then decide whether or not to turn him over to the United States. The U.S. government didn't even want that. Its "diplomacy" was deliberately designed to lead to war.

Revenge was the motive for the war. Although many people felt an emotional desire for revenge, the two principal reasons for war cannot be described in these terms. The first reason is that of imperial credibility. The United States is an empire, of a different kind from the Roman or the British, but still one that holds sway over much of the world through a combination of economic and military domination. In order to remain in power, an empire must show no weakness; it must crush any threat to its control. The last half of the Vietnam War, after the U.S. government realized there would be no political victory, was fought for credibility to show other countries the price of defiance. The need was all the greater with such a devastating attack in the center of imperial power. The second reason is leverage over the oil and natural gas of Central Asia. Afghanistan is the one country that the United States could control through which a pipeline can be run from those reserves to the Indian Ocean, for the rapidly growing Asian market. The war would provide an opportunity for that, as well as a chance to set up military bases in the former Soviet republics of the region.

The war was a humanitarian intervention as well as an attempt to get the terrorists. The food drops [in Afghanistan] were mere military propaganda—enough food for 37,500 people a day, if it was distributed, which it couldn't be—and they accompanied bombing that disrupted aid programs designed to feed millions. The lack of humanitarian intent was shown later by the U.S. government's ignoring a call by aid agencies and U.N. officials for a bombing halt so enough food could be trucked in. UNICEF estimated that because of the disruption of aid caused by the bombing and earlier the threat of bombing, as many as 100,000 more children might die in the winter. After the withdrawal of the Taliban, as much of the country collapsed into chaos and bandits started looting aid stores, the United States held up for almost a month proposals for a peacekeeping force, and didn't even pressure the Northern Alliance to restore order and facilitate aid, as aid workers were unable to reach at least one million people in desperate need.

The war was conducted by surgical strikes, minimizing collateral damage. There's no such thing as a surgical strike—the most precise weapons miss 20–30 percent of the time, and only 60 percent of the ordnance dropped on Afghanistan has been precision-guided. The United States has also used such devastating weapons as cluster bombs and daisy cutters, which by their nature are indiscriminate, so "collateral damage" cannot be controlled. Also, U.S. bombing campaigns generally deliberately target civilian infrastructure. In this case, there are reports of power stations, telephone exchanges, and even a major dam being destroyed, with potentially catastrophic effects. Totaling up all reports, including those from the foreign press, Professor Marc Herold of the University of New Hampshire estimated the number of civilians killed directly by bombs and bullets as of December 6, 2001 to be 3,767, a number he feels is, if anything, an underestimation. This is already greater than the number of innocents who died in the attacks on September 11, and it doesn't include the likely greater number who have died of indirect effects.

It was a war of civilization against barbarism. As if the above weren't enough, at the siege of Kunduz, where thousands of foreign fighters were trapped along with many thousands of Afghan Taliban fighters, Defense Secretary Donald Rumsfeld did everything short of calling for the foreigners to be killed. Later, a group of foreigners imprisoned in a fort and convinced they were going to be killed staged a rebellion. The fort was bombed and strafed by U.S. planes, even though later reports indicate that perhaps hundreds of the prisoners had their hands bound—this is almost certainly a war crime. At the same time, government officials and media pundits began calling for Osama bin Laden to be killed—even if he surrendered.

It was a war against terrorism. The Northern Alliance, which the United States has put in power over most of Afghanistan, is a bunch of terrorists, known for torture, killing civilians, and raping women. The United States harbors many terrorists, like Emanuel Constant of Haiti, a number of Cubans, and Henry Kissinger. It still runs its own terrorist training camp, the School of the Americas/Western Hemisphere Institute for Security Cooperation. It still supports Israeli state terrorism against the Palestinians. And it is committing state terrorism itself, by recklessly endangering civilians for its political goals.

The administration's primary motive has been to ensure the security of Americans. The war has greatly increased the risks to

Americans. By creating a tremendous pool of anger in the Muslim world, it is the ultimate recruiting vehicle for bin Laden, who is seen as a hero by many now, though he was ignored before. It was not even the best way to catch bin Laden, as pointed out above. Other measures decrease security as well. Calls to increase the scope of CIA operations and involve them more with criminals and terrorists seem to ignore the fact that it was just such CIA meddling that helped create the international Islamic extremist movement. Bush administration calls to sell weapons to countries that violate human rights destabilize the world. And missile defense, which would not have helped at all with an attack like this even if it was technically feasible, threatens to set off a new arms race. On the homefront, corporate profits and the ideology of free enterprise were more important to the administration than increasing security through the nationalization of airport security personnel, even though corporations have been found to be using convicted felons and paying barely over minimum wage, thus ensuring low motivation and incompetence. The profits of Bayer, the maker of Cipro, used to treat anthrax, were more important than ensuring a reasonably-priced supply of Cipro for people in case of a large-scale anthrax attack.

The attacks of September 11 united us together in a noble enterprise. Although many people did come together, the Bush administration tried to use that idea of unity to subvert democracy, even calling for Congress to give the president trade promotion authority (the right to present trade agreements "as is," so Congress can approve or disapprove but not amend) as part of the "war on terrorism." In the end, there was no unity; airline corporations were bailed out, while laid-off airline employees got nothing; the Republicans tried to give corporations a huge tax break in their economic stimulus package, while no provision was made to counter surging unemployment; and legislative aides on Capitol Hill got vastly better treatment during the anthrax scare than did postal workers.

This whole enterprise has also shed light on some longer-standing myths we hold about ourselves:

All sectors of society have an abiding commitment to civil liberties and due process of law. The USA PATRIOT Act allows law enforcement far greater power, including the right to search your house without notification. It can effectively deprive noncitizens of basic rights like habeas corpus. Attorney-client privilege has been breached in some cases. Many people have been held incommunicado for months in the ongoing investigation. Bush has even authorized the use of military tribunals, which can use secret evidence, convict on very low standards of evidence, and deny a defendant the right to choose a lawyer. The FBI has even considered sending detainees to other countries to be tortured. Although there is significant opposition to these threats to civil liberties and due process, it is not as yet very widespread.

We've made tremendous progress on racism. A majority of Americans now approve of racial profiling. There was a huge upsurge in hate crimes after September 11. And many people have openly expressed appallingly racist and even genocidal sentiments. Calls to nuke entire countries have been made. Although there is now a small group of (mostly younger) people largely free of racist sentiments, for the majority, the progress has mainly been in learning how to hide their racism.

We honor dissent and the right to free speech. Public discourse was characterized by an extreme overreaction to the small number of people who spoke against war. Several journalists have been fired, and many people subjected to death threats and other harassment. A rightwing foundation has brought out a report criticizing academia for not rallying round the flag even though the number of dissenters in academia were few and far between. With the constant demonization of dissent and misrepresentation of dissenters by elite institutions, it's not surprising that much of the populace has gone the same way—a recent CBS/NYT poll found 38 percent saying anti-war "marches and rallies" should not be allowed.

We have the freest and most independent media in the world. From the first hours, the mass media outdid any other sector of society in calling for blood. They showed, as they always do in wartime, a tremendous subservience to the government, with almost no dissenting points of view expressed.

When they did criticize government officials, it was almost always for not bombing enough. Most seriously, there was tremendous self-censorship. Numerous critical issues were covered hardly at all: the fact that a deal for extradition of bin Laden had been worked out; the fact that the United States had planned war against Afghanistan since before the attacks; the connection of oil with the war; and more. Worst was the persistent lack of attention to civilian casualties. Only a few incidents were even reported, and those were dismissed by constant repetition of Pentagon claims that they were "propaganda." As a result, many think that a handful of civilians were killed, whereas the truth is that thousands were. The government, not satisfied with this level of subservience, imposed unprecedented restrictions, not allowing any press pools until the end of November, allowing virtually no interviews with soldiers, and keeping the press from reporting even well known information. Some of the foreign press, whose reportage could not be controlled by such means, was treated more harshly. The U.S. government asked Qatar to censor al-Jazeera and later bombed its office in Kabul, as well as bombing civilian Afghan radio repeatedly, a war crime. The U.S. press also ridiculed and misrepresented the anti-war movement, insinuating that it had only slogans, not analysis; that it did not condemn the terrorist attacks; and, worst, that its solution was to "do nothing."

In fact, that was perhaps the biggest myth of the whole enterprise—that there was no other alternative, so we must either wreak destruction on Afghanistan or do nothing. Repeated efforts by the anti-war movement to indicate the foundations of a real solution—a genuine international investigation based on cooperation with not just governments but people, based on a dramatic change in U.S. policy in the Middle East to win over the "hearts and minds" of people there—were to little avail. These myths made a real difference. Although the majority of Americans have supported the supposed war on terrorism, their support has been based on a misunderstanding of how the war was being conducted, how much "collateral damage" there was, and what alternatives were possible.

The U.S. Role in the World Must Change

To have any chance of dealing with the problem of international terrorism, we must change the role of the United States in the world. In an essay entitled "The War Comes Home," published on the Web the day after the attacks, I wrote, "The main practitioner of attacks that either deliberately target civilians, or are so indiscriminate that it makes no difference, is no shadowy Middle Eastern terrorist, but our own government." These attacks run the gamut from direct bombing, as the United States has done in Iraq (on numerous occasions), Serbia, Sudan, Afghanistan, and other countries in the past ten years alone, to denying people access to the basic necessities of life. From the sanctions on Iraq, which have for years involved denying basic medical care to millions, to efforts to keep South Africa from providing affordable AIDS drugs to its citizens, the United States has killed countless civilians.

There is always a justification, as there is for any killing anywhere; for the sanctions on Iraq, it is the security of Iraq's neighbors, and for denying AIDS drugs, it is the need to maintain corporate profits. For the terrorists who attacked on September 11, it was the need to oppose U.S.-sanctioned murder and oppression in their part of the world. If "terrorism" is to be given an unbiased definition, it must involve the killing of noncombatants for political purposes, no matter who does it or what noble goals they proclaim.

When Madeleine Albright, then Secretary of State, went on 60 Minutes on May 12, 1996, Lesley Stahl said, referring to the sanctions on Iraq, "We have heard that a half million children have died. I mean, that's more children than died in Hiroshima. And, you know, is the price worth it?" Albright, not contesting the figure, replied, "I think this is a very hard choice, but the price—we think the price is worth it." That is the philosophy of terrorism. The people who crashed planes into the World Trade Center killed almost four thousand people because they resented U.S. domination of the Middle East. The U.S. government helped to kill a half million children in Iraq in order to preserve that domination.

It is the common fashion to dismiss such juxtapositions as

claims of "moral equivalence." In fact, that concept is irrelevant. Whether or not the U.S. government is "morally equivalent" to the terrorists, whatever that might mean, the point is that citizens of the United States have an obligation to oppose its crimes even before they would oppose the crimes of others over whom they have less control.

This does not mean efforts should not be made to stop terrorists of the ilk of Osama bin Laden. It simply means that terrorist efforts to stop them should not be made. The war on Afghanistan has been even worse—terrorist in its methods and designed primarily to project U.S. imperial power, not to stop the terrorists.

If Albright appears on *60 Minutes* again, this time she should be asked whether she thinks U.S. policy goals in the Middle East were also worth the deaths of thousands of Americans.

The War on Terrorism Is a Struggle for the Future Shape of the World

Gregory R. Copley

Strategic analyst, historian, and author Gregory R. Copley has worked in the defense analysis business for more than thirty years. As a consultant he has advised various governments, at the highest levels, on foreign policy and security issues. In 1972 he founded the Defense and Foreign Affairs group of publications, and he still acts as editor-in-chief for these publications.

In this analysis of the struggle against terror, Copley takes a broad strategic view of what he calls World War III. He compares the fight against Islamic terror to great historical events such as the fight against the Nazis in World War II. In this war, the terrorists are attempting to destroy the nation-state system and unite the Muslim world in the form of a Caliphate. The West, on the other hand, seeks a world of free trade and interaction between peoples, but with a large variety in social systems.

World War III began with the thunderclap impact of the terrorist attacks on the United States of America on September 11, 2001. It is a war of global dimension. It is a war which will continue until one bloc in the contest is defeated. It will continue until the completion of that defeat, now that it has been engaged in earnest, regardless of whether one side or the other unilaterally elects to waver or withdraw from the fight. It is a war which will be as different from World War II as World War II was different from the Great War: World War I. It is a war of psycho-politics and psychological strategy, and

---

Gregory R. Copley, "World War III: By Any Other Name," *Defense and Foreign Affairs Strategic Policy*, vol. 29, September 2001, pp. 4–7. Copyright © 2001 by The International Strategic Studies Association. Reproduced by permission of the author.

any attempt to address it in a 20th Century framework will merely make the conflict more protracted and costly.

But like World Wars I and II, the outcome of World War III will inevitably change the global geopolitical alignment of societies. Only one antagonist in this new war has been clearly identified: the United States. And should the US, through some change of political will or change of government, unwisely elect at some stage to retire from the fight, the war will continue in one form or another, and the US would ultimately be the loser. This is a war which will have moments of apparent quiet, like the "Phony War" which characterized the first months of World War II in 1939–40. But the new "phony war" periods will merely be times of discreet maneuvering in the psychopolitical arena, away from the physical imagery associated with "real war".

In that sense, it will be a war of protracted tensions, demanding patience and a constant vision of goals. . . .

A Recognition of War

The United States and, indeed, all the Western-oriented world, had, by September 11, 2001, been at war for more than a decade, but failed to recognize the fact, so relieved was it to have seen an end to the Cold War. Perhaps it would have been easier to have recognized the state of war had it been possible to identify the "enemy". Had it been recognized that a sovereign state had bombed the US Embassies in Dar-es Salaam, Tanzania, and Nairobi, Kenya, on August 7, 1998, then perhaps the impact would have been similar to the assassination of Archduke Francis Ferdinand of Austria-Este on June 28, 1914. [Even that assassination, a terrorist action, was unclear in its origins, and the response, World War I, was based on instinct rather than intelligence.]

Had it been recognized that the suicide bombing of the warship USS *Cole*, in Aden Harbor, Yemen, on October 12, 2000, was attributable to the orders of a sovereign state, the response would probably have been similar to that of the sinking of the RMS Lusitania on May 7, 1915: an incident which ultimately propelled a reluctant United States into war with the Triple Alliance powers.

The reality is that the coalition of forces which have been "waging war" against the US and the West for the past decade had been unable to attract the attention of their rival because they had lacked cohesion, lacked size and scope, and lacked focus. It seems apparent, now that they had for some years been attempting to goad the West into a response of such enormous magnitude that it would create a major schism, pitting the West against the entire Muslim world. Only by such an action could the moderate majority of the Muslim world be polarized away from the West and toward a radical Islamist (rather than truly Islamic) leadership. And only by some massive schism could the West itself be forced to regard the Muslim Ummah, or world, as an enemy, en bloc.

Viewed from this perspective, the resumption of the intifada—the uprising—in Israel and the Palestinian Authority (PA) territories makes sense. Why else would the sponsors of the intifada throw away all of the political, social and economic gains they had made, merely to deliberately taunt and force Israel into a military response which could jeopardize any hope of a peaceful settlement in the Middle East?

And yet none of this disturbed the equilibrium of a West bent on luxuriating in the "peace dividend" erroneously thought to have existed at the end of the Cold War. The attacks against the established moderate societies in the Middle East, Africa, the Balkans and elsewhere were scarcely noticed. No pattern was detected; all were rationalized as sporadic reflections of local issues and isolated motivations. And, indeed, those bent against the West were divided and differed greatly in their goals and methods. Many anti-Western or anti-Israeli activists themselves would not have recognized that they were part of a pattern, gradually coalescing.

What has finally happened is that the numerous anti-Western Islamists have been forcibly united to the point—with the September 11, 2001, attacks on the United States—where they represented an identifiable threat which the West itself could no longer ignore. The attacks were clearly, in part, designed to galvanize the various anti-Western elements and to unite them, as well as to polarize the West.

A Failed Attempt

The attacks did gain Western attention; they did galvanize many of the anti-Western elements. But they did not achieve their purpose. While shaking the Muslim world, they failed to unite all Muslims in condemnation of the West; nor did the events cause the West to be alienated from, or attack, the Muslim Ummah as a whole.

Battle lines were drawn, and the scope of the conflict became clear as a global war. But by failing to polarize the Muslim and non-Muslim worlds, the sponsors of the war placed themselves at a significant disadvantage in the long term. An alliance of forces including the industrialized (or pro-industrialized) world and the moderate Muslim world can, if it sustains its focus and cohesion, more than match a radical bloc of states and movements.

It will therefore be the goal of the radical bloc to continue to destabilize its opponents, to disrupt its cohesion, and to attempt continuously to bring about the disaffection from the West of the moderate Muslim populations, helping them to force their leaders into abandoning the West. Again, seen in hindsight, the destruction by the Afghan Taliban movement of the giant Buddhist statues of Bamiyan, early in 2000, was part of the attempt to create an irreversible schism between the Muslim and non-Muslim worlds. It failed, but it was part of the strategy.

A World War

It can be argued that the new conflict is of global dimension—because of the worldwide dispersal of the terrorist forces—but is it a "world war"? It is a war unlike any other, and it is—to a greater extent than any other—a war of politics and psycho-politics as much as it is a war of physical force. It is a world war in that, on the one hand, it was initiated by people who wish to see the entire Western world collapse, and for a fundamentalist pseudo-theocratic system to reign supreme. That goal is no less ludicrous than the aspirations of Adolph Hitler and his Nazis to dominate the world, or for Napoleon to envision global dominance.

The aspirations of Osama bin Laden, the Taliban, and

Sudan's Hassan al-Turabi, are to destroy the nation-state system as it has existed and evolved since the Treaty (or Peace) of Westphalia of October 24, 1648. They are, in that sense, anti-nationalists, currently operating as trans-nationalists, but wishing to re-focus power in a form of Caliphate [the unified rule over the Islamic world during the Middle Ages].

However, on the other hand, it is a global war of a different type for the West, as it should be for all pro-modernist states, if they wish to survive and prosper. For them it is a chance, on a global scale, to redraw the alignments of states, ensuring in the future a structure between societies which entails less friction and greater interaction. The "new" modern society is also dispensing to some extent with the nation-state as it was defined by the Peace of Westphalia. However, it does not wish to replace it with a focus of power in absolutism, but rather to replace it with a more fluid and less centralized structure.

Neither protagonist in this new war can move toward these respective ends smoothly, but the bloc which is now categorized as "terrorist" (because that is the method it employs to achieve its ends) aims at destruction leading to centralism, while the "West" (a poor name for the global grouping of industrial, trading and essentially representative-government societies) aims at an evolutionary process of construction leading to decentralization.

Assuming the West maintains its focus and will, its superior wealth and technology should enable a reasonably efficient (but by no means clean, clear or bloodless) defeat of the "terrorists" over a period of years. The "terrorists", by virtue of their smaller numbers and lower technology, must rely on "will" and, literally, on terror tactics to divide their opponents and to cause panic, paralysis, economic stagnation, despair and mistrust in their enemies' societies.

The attempt on October 2, 2001, by the Taliban/bin Laden forces to escalate tensions, and perhaps create war, between India and Pakistan (by the suicide bombing of the Assembly in Indian-occupied Jammu & Kashmir, killing 38), was an astute example of how a low-cost stratagem could help stave off defeat. Had India succumbed to the emotional reaction of its public and invaded Pakistan as a response to the incident, it could have jeopardized the Western ability to inject forces via Pakistan into Afghanistan to attack the Taliban and bin Laden.

What will be more difficult for the West than attacking and destroying many of the terrorist groups and their sponsors will be in maintaining a unity of purpose in actually redefining the world, "post–World War III". It is only possible to achieve "victory" by recognizing that this is a conflict for the future shape of the world, and thereby recognizing that it is a contest not just against terrorism but against the ancient regime of the world itself. The Taliban and bin Laden will be the forgotten triggers, just as Gavrilo Princip, the man who shot Archduke Ferdinand in 1914, has become a footnote of history. But only if US President [George W.] Bush can sustain a campaign over many years to truly eradicate the focus of the anti-Western movement, and then build a coalition of trust which would break down barriers between today's West and tomorrow's, which could include all those states who wish for a stable, peaceful, prosperous and free-moving system of trade and interaction.

Of course, to achieve this, Mr Bush must, with his allies, move to suppress the immediate threat and at the same time ensure the survival of his own political position.

The Nature of the New War

If there is an evolution in warfare's underlying fundamentals then it is that success should increasingly lie in the application of wisdom to defeat ignorance. Such a statement is presumed to favor the cosmopolitan, educated and technocratic West. However, this is not necessarily the case, as the defeat of the Roman Empire exemplified. Wealth, safety and stability encourage complacency, insensitivity, arrogance and over-confidence. A poor, ill-educated and insular opponent may, by virtue of the self-knowledge of his paucity of strengths, devote greater care to his strategies and tactics. That is the essence of asymmetrical warfare.

[Ancient Chinese military theorist] Sun-tzu said: "To fight and conquer in all your battles is not supreme excellence; supreme excellence consists in breaking the enemy's resistance without fighting."

It will be the goal of the Taliban and bin Laden's organizations, as well as their allies, to fight as little or as sporadically as possible (or necessary), and to let their enemies exhaust themselves on the battlefield. If at all possible, they will continue to undertake distracting attacks on civilian targets and high economic value targets far from the initial combat front in Afghanistan. They have a great ability to "break the enemy's resistance" with very little actual fighting. They also believe that they have a greater will to fight a longer war than does the West.

By its nature, Western operational strategies will embrace concepts of humanitarianism which dictate some of the military doctrine employed. The Taliban, bin Laden, Iraq and Iran will not be guided by the same approach to humanitarianism, and their operating doctrine will thus be more flexible, and will manipulate the psychological imagery of the war, either to create fear or sympathy. As the war becomes protracted, costly and frustrating, there will be many in the West who will demand a unilateral end to the fighting and insist on unilateral—even unsought—compromise by the West. These voices will be from those who judge their opponents by the standards of Western logic, disregarding the logic, goals and attitudes of the foe. These voices will be from those who fail to see, or who forget, the ultimate goals of the conflict on both sides: to shape the future of the world.

Psychological and Military Strategies

If the civilized world of moderate societies is to prevail, then the leaders and governments of those states will need to devise ongoing psychological strategies to educate and motivate their own societies. They will need answers for those baying for "peace" when the need for patience and perseverance is at its greatest.

At the same time, those conducting military operations will need to move cautiously, to preserve a wellspring of strength for a protracted conflict. They will need also the ability to accept significant changes in military doctrine, technology and structure to fight different kinds of wars. On the one hand, there will remain a need to ensure the lack of efficacy of weapons of mass destruction (WMD), delivered by ballistic missiles. These remain a threat for the foreseeable decades. The denial of viability of these weapons—which can only be achieved by continuing to pursue operational capability of theater-oriented and global anti-ballistic missile systems—will limit the capability of "gunpowder" states, such as Iraq, Iran and North Korea.

On the other hand, there will be a greater than ever need to marry the West's superiority of logistical capability with technology and the broadening of numbers of highly-trained rapidly-deployable infantrymen.

For the terrorism-oriented forces opposing them, there will inevitably be the need to either avoid reliance on technological systems which create detectable signatures, or to find ways to use the West's own technologies to feint, ghost or circumvent Western detection. Ultimately, however, the terrorist-oriented forces can, for the most part, be gradually starved of the weapons they need to conduct a strategically viable war. Their approach to conflict does not favor industrialization; therefore they must rely on industrial states to provide weapons, ammunition, communications systems, computers, and so on. Their approach to governance does not favor long-term control over stable, viable agricultural territory; therefore, they eventually become starved of food.

State Sponsors of Terrorism

In all areas, then, they are dependent upon their enemies for sustenance. But that leads us to the more critical challenges of the new war: the states which sponsor the terrorists. Here, the West is also hampered by its desire for clear imagery in defining its opponents. It has, until now, failed to adopt the mind-set which comprehends the pattern of tactical, ad hoc alliances or mutual animosities which govern the way in which anti-Western forces have operated, particularly since the end of the Cold War. Iran and the forces around Osama bin Laden, for example have diametrically opposed views on the dispute underway in the Russian autonomous republic of

Chechnya. And yet the bin Laden forces can and do cooperate with Iran's surrogate HizbAllah terrorist and guerilla forces, operating mainly in the anti-Israeli war. There are many instances where common hatred of an enemy dictates that groups lend support to each other when on other occasions they would be at war with each other.

The states which most critically—and at a formal governmental level—have supported terrorism in recent years, and who are of major concern at present, are Iran, Iraq, Syria and Sudan. There have been numerous other governments which have, at some levels, also supported or assisted terrorism without it necessarily being state policy. But the fountainheads of state support for terrorism are Iran, its surrogate Syria, and Iraq. But in all of these states, it is an unrepresentative leadership, rather than the populace, which is to blame.

Undertaking a military operation to remove this threat is not the West's best option, however. Such actions—"20th Century thinking"—would be costly and irresponsible. What is necessary, by identifying the reality that the populations of Iran, Iraq and Syria are as much victims of terrorism as the West, is that the populations be meaningfully assisted to remove the leaders who have been imposed upon them, and given the ability to choose governments which will help them integrate with the rest of the world.

Past Western attempts (often led by the US Central Intelligence Agency) at supporting indigenous groups to oust the Iranian clerics have been poorly conceived and have failed. A far more sophisticated, empathetic and culturally educated approach would be necessary if the West truly wished to see a change in the leaderships in those hostile countries. Ultimately, the goal should not be merely to change hostile governments for friendly ones, but rather to assist populations in getting the governments which will best serve them, relying on the underlying desire of most people to live in societies at peace and harmony with other societies.

But whatever else happens, there will be no end to the war until the leaderships and governments of Iran, Iraq and Syria—at least—are exchanged for governments more representative of their populations.

The Desired Outcome

Grand strategy objectives must be envisioned in conceptual terms; idealized, perhaps. What must be sought is an ideal. We ultimately must live with the compromises to that ideal, but without first having an ideal, we cannot have an acceptable compromise.

The anti-Western elements of the new war have, for the most part, identified their goals as a world in which the entire Muslim Ummah is united around a single Caliphate which eschews any Western influence, and a world in which the West (as we have defined that bloc) is reduced somehow to nothing, or is removed from consideration. It is a vague goal, based largely on destruction and subjugation.

The Western elements of this new war have the opportunity to define their grand strategy objectives as including all states in an equitable trading and social system which allows for peaceful competition and interaction, while also allowing for great variations in societal cultures and beliefs. Under such a goal, there is no reason why, for example, the "West" should not include all of the states of the Americas, all of Western, Eastern and Southern Europe, all of the Caucasus, Russia, China, both Koreas and Japan, Australasia, the ASEAN [Association of SouthEast Asian Nations] states, India and Pakistan, virtually all of Africa and the Middle East, including Israel. . . . States such as Iran, Iraq, Syria, Sudan, etc., can, upon reformation, also be brought into this new alignment.

Chapter 3

Domestic Antiterrorism Efforts

Intelligence and Law Enforcement Are Key Tools in Fighting Terrorism

Jeffrey D. Simon

In the following selection, Jeffrey D. Simon argues that improving law enforcement and intelligence are the best methods for countering terrorism. He maintains that intelligence agents and law enforcement officials have already prevented many terrorists attacks. Because such successes often are not reported in the press, the public does not realize how effective these methods are in fighting terrorism. According to Simon, a major improvement would be increased sharing of intelligence between countries. Terrorist groups often make foolish errors that allow law enforcement officials to prevent attacks. In order to exploit these mistakes more fully, intelligence operations must be improved. All nations are now potential targets of attack by international terrorist groups. To counter this threat, agencies must be more willing to give their foreign counterparts access to intelligence about terrorist groups. Simon is a foreign policy consultant and writer who has published opinion pieces in the *New York Times*, the *Los Angeles Times*, and *USA Today*. He is the author of *The Terrorist Trap*, from which this excerpt was taken.

It used to be said that the two things in life everybody could be sure of were death and taxes. A third, though, could be added to the list. Any speech on terrorism that calls for vigorous action against all terrorists will be guaranteed enthusiastic applause. But combating terrorism requires more than just rhetoric. It requires careful assessment of the costs and benefits of various actions and a concentration on those options that promise the most payoffs.

Intelligence and Law Enforcement

The least publicized, yet most effective, part of the counterterrorist efforts of most countries lies in the areas of intelligence and law enforcement. These are the people who are on the front lines, yet whose quiet work usually gets lost in the hoopla that surrounds the more publicized military, economic, and diplomatic measures.

Many terrorist incidents have been prevented due to the efforts of intelligence agents and analysts, as well as law enforcement personnel in the United States and abroad. Most of these are not publicized in order to prevent compromising intelligence or police methods. Among those that have become known was a plot in the mid-1980s to blow up the American embassy in Rome. This failed after Swiss police arrested a Lebanese man at the Zurich airport and found two pounds of explosives in his possession, as well as a ticket to Rome and an address there. Police found two more pounds of explosives in a locker at the Zurich railroad station. Italian authorities were alerted and they arrested seven Lebanese students who had ties to pro-Iranian Shiite extremists. A search of the students' apartments found a detailed map of the U.S. embassy, notes on vulnerable access points, and arrows pointing to the positions of the guards, television cameras, and concrete blocks. In another case, West German police discovered lists of clubs frequented by U.S. troops, barracks, and the residences and offices of military commanders in a Red Army Faction terrorist safe-house in Frankfurt in 1984.

Among the potential terrorist attacks thwarted by good law enforcement work in the United States was the arrest of a group of Islamic militants in 1993 for plotting to blow up the United Nations headquarters and other targets in New York, and the apprehension of Japanese Red Army terrorist Yu Kikumura in 1987 on the New Jersey Turnpike before he could initiate a series of planned bombings in New York City. Another example was the arrest of members of the El

Rukn street gang in Chicago in 1986 after they purchased an inert light antitank weapon from undercover FBI agents. The gang allegedly planned a terrorist attack within the United States in exchange for funding from Libya. In August 1991, the FBI discovered and prevented a plot by the Palestine Liberation Front to commit a terrorist attack against the Kuwaiti mission to the United Nations and/or the ambassador to that mission in New York.

Exploiting Terrorists' Mistakes

Sometimes the terrorists make foolish mistakes that lead to serious blows to their organization. One of the World Trade Center bombers [in the first attempt to bomb the World Trade Center in 1993] was caught, leading to other arrests, when he tried to obtain a refund on the rental van that carried the explosives into the trade center. In another case, Spanish police reportedly gained possession of an address book that was mistakenly left in a telephone booth in Barcelona by a member of the Basque [an ethnic group in Spain] separatist group ETA. The Spanish authorities provided information to French police, who, in March 1992, raided a high-level ETA meeting in the Basque region of southwestern France. The leader of the group, Francisco Mugica Garmendia, was arrested, along with two of his top aides, including the ETA's chief bomb maker. Several other ETA members were captured in the raid, while Spanish police arrested five more suspected ETA guerrillas in northern Spain. The police and intelligence breakthrough came on the eve of the World's Fair in Seville and the Summer Olympics in Barcelona.

The International Criminal Police Organization (Interpol) has also provided valuable assistance to countries through its communications network, computerized files, and agents throughout the world. In one case in the late 1970s, the Beirut [Lebanon] office of Interpol alerted its counterpart in Nicosia, Cyprus, about a time bomb that was aboard an airliner bound for Rome. Interpol-Nicosia informed the pilot, who then returned the plane to the ground where the bomb was discovered and removed. Interpol's role in counterterrorist matters was improved greatly in 1984, when member nations passed a resolution that changed Interpol's definition of terrorism from a "political" act to a "criminal" act. This allowed members to cooperate fully on terrorist investigations, whereas previously they could not do so under Interpol's constitutional ban on involvement in political, military, religious, or racial matters. Interpol subsequently created a special unit to collect information on terrorists and terrorist acts and provide this information to Interpol members.

The potential for further international cooperation in intelligence on terrorism is higher today than at any previous time. The end of the Cold War has removed many barriers to East-West cooperation on several issues, including political and economic affairs. Cooperation on counterterrorist intelligence matters with the newly formed nations of the former Soviet Union and Eastern Europe should be pursued while the spirit of cooperation is still there on other issues. The United States and other Western nations should also take advantage of the increased awareness level of governments throughout the world concerning the prospects for more terrorism to arise from extremist religious, ethnic, and nationalist groups in the post–Cold War era—as well as from old and new state-sponsors of terrorism—to form new networks of information and knowledge about terrorist group developments.

Sharing Intelligence Vital in Fight Against Terrorism

Establishing an expanded and continually updated network among nations for sharing intelligence on terrorism would yield many benefits. Since no government can monitor, track, and follow up on developments concerning every terrorist group worldwide, a pooling of resources would provide potentially important information. "The issues of intelligence are critical, in terms of trying to determine where people are moving to, what their relationships are," said Robert McGuire, police commissioner of New York City in the late 1970s and early 1980s. For countries such as the United States, whose citizens and symbols are present in virtually every country around the world and who are prone to terrorist attack by a wide variety of groups, there is a definite need to know about the latest developments within terrorist groups in other countries, recent information on the movements of suspected terrorists, discovery of weapons in safehouses, and so forth. The more that counterterrorist intelligence and police officials from different countries are in continual contact with each other, the more likely it is some incidents may be averted.

A major obstacle, however, to establishing such a network is the understandable concern that sharing secret information with other governments may compromise one's own intelligence-gathering methods or even one's informants and operatives around the world. "It takes a while for people to feel comfortable sharing intelligence," recalled former Secretary of State George Shultz. "And to a certain extent, since valuable intelligence in terrorism involves very delicate techniques of gathering information, there is an uneasiness about it in case it gets out. You can kill somebody by getting it out."

Indeed, the tendency for U.S. politics and government to be beset by numerous leaks, including information relevant to national security matters, greatly troubled other governments. Shultz recalled that foreign governments were hesitant at times to cooperate with the United States in intelligence matters "because we're so leaky. And our Congress and our press insist that everybody has a right to know everything. But if we have a right to know your sources of intelligence, then you're not going to get anybody to tell you something. We had that problem all the time. We wrestled with it."

There is also a reluctance among counterterrorist officials to share information with each other in the general international meetings that are occasionally held to address the problem of international terrorism. "As far as I know, specialized intelligence will never be shared in a large assembly," observed Constantine Melnik, a former French government official who held office during the Algerian civil war [in which Algerians fought for independence from France] and its associated terrorism during the late 1950s and early 1960s. "You will never tell in a large assembly that you have information about one specific German terrorist who is coming to France, and in a given time, in a given little village, and that we have located the village and we are interested to find out when it is the best time to arrest him. This kind of information will never be given on a large scale. . . . And you don't tell about your own techniques."

It is therefore critical that counterterrorist officials and specialists build trust among each other so they can work together to uncover potential terrorist activity and follow up on the movements of suspected terrorists. "I think this has to be done on a very specific level," said Melnik. "If you need the cooperation on the level of criminal polices, then it is very important to let the criminal polices [from different countries] meet together and find out the necessary measures [to take]." The same is true for counterterrorist specialists in aviation and embassy security, terrorist group psychology, and experts on terrorist weapons and tactics.

The Threat of Weapons of Mass Destruction

The area of terrorism in which the role of intelligence will become most critical in the years ahead will be in the potential for terrorists to utilize weapons of mass destruction. Since the repercussions of a terrorist incident with nuclear, chemical, or biological weapons would be much greater than with conventional weapons, in terms of casualties, panic, fear, and other effects, the highest priority will need to be given to preventing even a single incident.

Since all nations could conceivably be affected by terrorists with nuclear, chemical, or biological agents—whereas a hijacking, a conventional bombing, or an assassination could be seen as more isolated—there should be an even higher incentive for governments to cooperate in this area. Among the intelligence indicators that should be conveyed to all other nations and joint efforts undertaken to track them down would be the suspicious theft of certain hazardous or scientific materials that could be used to build nuclear, chemical, or biological weapons; the recruitment of nuclear or biological specialists into the ranks of terrorist groups; or the discovery of documents that would lead one to suspect that a terrorist group was planning or thinking about using these types of weapons. This is an issue in terrorism that needs to be nipped in the bud, so to speak, or at least maintained at a continually heightened level of vigilance to try to prevent such a catastrophe from occurring.

Covert Operations: High Risk but High Reward

While intelligence-gathering and analysis hold the most promise for making gains in preventing some terrorist incidents, covert operations hold much higher risks. Counterterrorism efforts would be undoubtedly enhanced if terrorist groups could be penetrated by government agents or informers. This would not only yield information about planned attacks, but would also provide opportunities to confuse and trick the terrorists by providing misleading and false information. However, penetrating a terrorist group is difficult since many terrorist groups consist of just a few members, and in some cases, such as in Lebanon, are held together by family ties. Furthermore, some terrorist groups require new members to participate in a violent act to prove their loyalty, thereby negating infiltration by a police or government agent.

The use of surrogates, that is, local indigenous groups, to carry out disruptive operations against terrorists has the advantage of utilizing people who are probably familiar with the villages, towns, and possibly even the movements of various terrorist groups. However, the major pitfall is that it may be difficult to control the activities of any foreign group, as the United States painfully learned in Lebanon in 1985. President Reagan had earlier signed a "finding" that authorized the CIA to train Lebanese units for possible preemptive attacks against terrorists. But the U.S.-trained unit then hired mercenaries, who went on an unauthorized operation that resulted in a car bombing at the Beirut suburb apartment of Hizballah [a radical Islamic group] leader Sheikh Mohammed Hussein Fadlallah. Eighty people were killed, and Fadlallah escaped the assassination attempt. Following this fiasco, President Reagan rescinded the finding.

The most widely debated issue concerning covert operations against terrorists is that of assassination. Each time there is a major terrorist incident involving Americans, there are usually calls by various people to repeal the executive order that prohibits the U.S. government from engaging in assassination. This is understandable, since paying back terrorists by the same means that they use would seem to be poetic justice. The Israelis have used assassinations to retaliate against terrorists, including the hunting down of the Black September members responsible for the massacre at the 1972 Olympic Games in Munich; the killing of Abu Jihad, the military commander of the PLO, in 1988; and the killing of Sheikh Abbas Musawi, the head of Hizballah, in an aerial bombing of a convoy he was traveling with in southern Lebanon in 1992.

However, there are several reasons why assassination is not a wise counterterrorist option. First, it does not reduce or eliminate the terrorist threat, since there are others who will take the place of the slain terrorist leader or member. It also creates new martyrs for the terrorist group and provides additional fuel to fan the passions and anger of its supporters. This can lead to further terrorist attacks, as occurred in 1992 when Islamic Jihad claimed responsibility for a car bombing of the Israeli embassy in Buenos Aires [Argentina] following the Israeli attack on Musawi.

Allowing the assassination of terrorists also reduces a government to the level of the terrorists and takes away any potential moral argument that may be used against terrorism. The terrorists thus succeed in bringing the government into its violent playing field. There is also the risk of killing the wrong person. Furthermore, since there is no consensus on what exactly constitutes a "terrorist," there could be room for misuse of the "right" to engage in assassination if it becomes part of a government's counterterrorist strategy. Various foreign individuals or leaders might be targeted under the guise of being "terrorists," when in fact it is for other reasons—political, personal, ideological—that they are marked for death. As national security scholar Loch Johnson writes, "Almost always, [assassination] remains an unworthy, illegal and, for that matter, impractical approach to America's international problems."

Domestic Antiterrorism Measures May Endanger Civil Liberties

Robert Dreyfus

Robert Dreyfus is an investigative journalist based in Virginia. In the following article, he describes the efforts of police departments around the country to create or rebuild intelligence and antiterrorism units. Civil rights groups view these developments with alarm. They believe these tactics will create a social environment similar to the 1960s, when civil rights leaders and other dissidents were monitored by the FBI. Despite these concerns, plans for monitoring dissident groups are being crafted. Attorney General John Ashcroft hopes to create a network of local police departments and federal authorities to facilitate such monitoring. Dreyfus fears that these monitoring efforts will last a long time and will inevitably lead to abuses.

Col. David Mitchell, superintendent of the Maryland State Police, is sitting at the end of a big conference table at police headquarters near Baltimore. Mitchell, a lawyer and thirty-one-year veteran of Maryland law enforcement, is talking about how terrorism has added a new mission for his officers since September 11. "After 9/11 we found out how many things we needed to know," says Mitchell, beefy and bespectacled under a full head of gray hair. "How many and where is every mosque in the state of Maryland? And every synagogue. And every airport and every runway. And every cropduster."

Within weeks of the attacks, says Mitchell, his organization expanded its intelligence unit, putting it on round-the-clock duty. The state police strengthened its already close

Robert Dreyfus, "The Cops Are Watching You," *Nation*, vol. 274, June 3, 2002, pp. 12–17. Copyright © 2002 by The Nation Company, Inc. Reproduced by permission.

relations with the FBI's Baltimore field office, and brought in a retired bureau terrorism expert to head its antiterrorism squad. The police also established the Maryland Intelligence Network to improve the flow of information between the FBI and county police departments across the state. The intelligence unit, which already had five officers with top-secret national security clearances, is being reinforced with other cleared officers, and Mitchell himself is in the process of receiving clearance to handle classified information from the FBI and the CIA.

What's happening in Maryland—based on interviews with the FBI in Baltimore, federal officials and state and local police officials nationwide—is a microcosm of a national trend.

Strengthening Police Intelligence Units

From New York to Chicago, from Florida to California, police departments are creating, rebuilding or strengthening intelligence units and antiterrorism squads. It's a trend that began slowly in the 1990s, after the first World Trade Center attack and the Oklahoma City bombing, but it has accelerated sharply—with major pushes from the FBI and the Justice Department—since September 2001. Some of the momentum is coming from police departments, responding to the new threat of terrorism and taking the opportunity to expand their powers. And some of it is coming from the Feds, in an effort to create "a seamless web" (in the words of Attorney General John Ashcroft) uniting local law enforcement, the FBI and the US intelligence community. A little-noticed provision of the USA Patriot Act, which passed Congress in fall 2001, requires the FBI and CIA to train state and local police to handle national security information.

Ironically, all this is occurring in the complete absence of any actual terrorist activity. In Maryland, FBI and police officials could not identify even one recorded incident of terrorism in the state. And the same is true elsewhere. Chicago, for instance, which is in the process of substantially relaxing restrictions on police surveillance activity, has experienced zero incidents of terrorism since the 1970s, when Puerto Rican independence activists set off a bomb in the city. And, according to both Chicago Police Department and FBI officials, not a single incident of terrorism has been prevented, either. "We've arrested people on anthrax hoaxes and bomb scares," says Pat Camden, spokesman for the CPD. But incidents? Zilch.

Still, since September 11 the Maryland State Police are spending more and more time preparing to track potential terrorists, from international, Al Qaeda-style suspects to a wide range of home-grown groups that, they believe, might be prone to violence. With expanded powers—in March, Mitchell led the charge when the Maryland state legislature passed antiterrorism measures that mimicked the expanded wiretap and surveillance provisions of the USA Patriot Act—the police are building files on potential terrorist organizations, both in-state and across the country. "We read their literature, we interview people who've attended their rallies," Mitchell says. "A lot of stuff we collect, it's off the Internet." And, he says, when the potential for violence suggests that it's necessary, the police infiltrate organizations and develop informants inside them. When I interviewed him, it was only days before a major protest against the International Monetary Fund in nearby Washington. "I'll have troops down there," Mitchell said. "We know there's a history of groups that are hellbent on violence, and we've got some intelligence activity going on there, too. We're keeping our ear to the ground."

Civil Liberties Groups Concerned About Police Powers

Mitchell, blunt-spoken and direct, says the state police are well aware of the public's sensitivity about police intelligence. "To a lot of people it conjures up John Lennon files and Red Squads," he says. "It's a fine line, and I'm very familiar with constitutional guarantees." That police might violate those guarantees is a longstanding concern of the American Civil Liberties Union, which opposed the Maryland antiterrorism law, and of other civil liberties advocates, who worry that police might conflate efforts against criminal terrorists with moves against rambunctious protesters and noisy dissidents, especially in cases where civil disobedience shades into window-breaking, spray-painting and vandalism. At the very least, says Gregory Nojeim of the ACLU's Washington office, police antiterrorism units tend to monitor protected, free-speech activities of opposition groups and those with unpopular views. At worst, they can begin to repress them.

"They're going to start reviving the Red Squads," predicts Michael Ratner of the Center for Constitutional Rights, referring to police operations that moved from targeting leftists to harassing civil rights and dissident groups before being shut down in the 1970s after abuses came to light. The FBI was forced to close down its Cointelpro operation, which spied on antiwar protesters and the New Left and often worked closely with the Red Squads.

The post-September 11 resurgence of police intelligence is too new for there to be evidence of abuses, but recent news from Denver, Colorado, shows what can happen. There, the ACLU revealed in March that since 1999 the police have maintained intelligence dossiers on 3,200 people in 208 organizations, from globalization protesters to the American Friends Service Committee, and from Amnesty International to the Chiapas Coalition and the American Indian Movement. "Individuals who are not even suspected of a crime and organizations that don't have a criminal history are labeled criminal extremists," says Mark Silverstein, legal director of the ACLU of Colorado.

Joint Terrorism Task Forces

Mitchell plans to travel to New York City to learn how police officials there have built the most formidable intelligence and antiterrorism squad in the nation. In fall 2001 New York hired David Cohen, a thirty-six-year veteran of the CIA and former chief of its covert operations wing, to run its intelligence unit. "I'd like to duplicate New York City here," Mitchell says. Meanwhile, Mitchell is playing a key role in Maryland's fledgling FBI Joint Terrorism Task Force (JTTF).

A couple of exits around the Maryland beltway from the State Police office, just off Security Boulevard, sits the large, squat building that houses the Baltimore field office of the

FBI and its 200 special agents. In the lobby, no one has gotten around to putting up a picture of the new FBI director, but hanging in an office is a worn-looking photograph of J. Edgar Hoover, who ran the Palmer raids in the 1920s and who headed the FBI for half a century. Inside, Mike Clemens is looking for real estate. Clemens, a veteran FBI agent who arrived in Baltimore just in time for September 11, began assembling Maryland's JTTF within weeks of the attacks.

Begun in Chicago and New York in the 1980s, JTTFs proliferated in the 1990s, growing to about three dozen by 2001. In the wake of September 11, [Attorney General John] Ashcroft and FBI Director Robert Mueller announced that all fifty-six FBI field offices would have a JTTF in place within a year. Modeled on antidrug task forces that began in the 1980s, the JTTFs were designed to bring state-of-the-art investigative techniques and technology to state and local police and a wide range of federal agencies, under the leadership of the FBI, in a mission aimed at both international and domestic terrorism.

In an interview, Clemens offered a rare glimpse into the scope and makeup of one of the FBI's terrorism task forces. He currently oversees three squads of ten FBI agents each: one dealing with international terrorism, one domestic terrorism and one cyberterrorism and computer crimes. The Maryland JTTF unites the FBI with police departments around the state; it includes officers from the Maryland State Police; from the city of Baltimore; from Baltimore, Montgomery, Prince Georges, Anne Arundel and Howard counties; and from the Immigration and Naturalization Service, Customs, the Secret Service, the Internal Revenue Service, the Bureau of Alcohol, Tobacco and Firearms, and other agencies, for a total of fifty to sixty full-time antiterrorist specialists. The real estate that Clemens needs is an off-site operations center for the task force, one that will include a large training facility for Maryland police officers.

The War on Terrorism Will Last a Long Time

"It's very obvious now, as reflected by President Bush's war on terrorism, that this effort is going to go on for a long time as a substantial, investigative effort," says Clemens. Like Mitchell, Clemens forthrightly acknowledges that domestic antiterrorism investigations could easily run afoul of Americans' civil liberties if the FBI and police are not careful, especially when it comes to protest groups. "There's a fine line," he says. "There has to be a reasonable indication that they are involved in violent activity or subversive activity that would rise to a level of a violation of the law." Then he catches himself at the use of "subversive." "Well, not subversive, but violent," he adds. "Are they just a radical group that does a lot of yabbering, exercising their First Amendment rights, or is it more?"

To determine which, the FBI—working in conjunction with state and local police—often gathers a significant amount of information on groups that end up having no proclivity toward violence, Clemens says. "We have general intelligence files on domestic terrorist groups," he says. "There are all sorts of those files. And again, you get into that fine line. We identify a group, develop sources inside it. Maybe we make fifteen contacts or more over a period of six months, and if they are all negative, we just leave them alone."

Meanwhile, across Maryland, police departments are building intelligence units and cementing ties to the FBI. In Baltimore, the police have added more officers and money to the intelligence unit. The city hired a retired FBI agent with antiterrorism experience as a consultant on intelligence matters and posted intelligence officers from the Baltimore Police Department to New York and Washington. In Montgomery County, which abuts Washington, "quite a bit has changed for us," says Deputy Police Chief Rob Barnhouse. He adds that "everybody in our department since 9/11 has responsibility for homeland security," feeding into a five-person intelligence squad and the county's permanent liaison with the ME. In Baltimore County the antiterrorism unit is tracking groups from the Ku Klux Klan to globalization activists. "We never like to talk about the intelligence unit," says Bill Toohey, a spokesman for the county police. "It just monitors things."

The most significant federal effort to prod police into

paying attention to terrorism and political violence began in the 1990s under Attorney General Janet Reno. To induce state and local governments to cooperate, the Justice Department offered financial aid; currently there is $445 million in the pot. Since September 11 that effort has accelerated dramatically, and now Ashcroft and White House homeland security czar Tom Ridge are pledging a tenfold increase in federal subsidies to police for antiterrorism. Ridge is asking for $3.5 billion next year for local police, fire and emergency services—on top of what cities, and local police, are spending themselves. According to the US Conference of Mayors, just 200 cities will spend $2.6 billion by the end of 2002 in security costs related to antiterrorism. That, in turn, has created a bonanza for private industry to supply goods and services to police departments. At the mayors' conference in Washington in January, eager vendors were everywhere displaying their wares, including sophisticated intelligence software.

Under the Justice Department program each state was asked to conduct a county-by-county assessment of potential terrorist threats in order to qualify for the federal largesse. In each city and county local police were required to identify up to fifteen groups or individuals called potential threat elements (PTEs). The Justice Department helpfully points out that the motivations of the PTEs could be "political, religious, racial, environmental [or] special interest." At a stroke, the Justice Department prompted 17,000 state and local police departments to begin monitoring radicals.

The initial response was modest; by September 2001 only one state—Utah—had qualified. But since September relentless pressure from Ashcroft has brought most states up to speed.

In Maryland, according to Don Lumpkins of the Maryland Emergency Management Agency, after an eighteen-month effort the police in Baltimore, Annapolis and twenty-three counties have come up with at least a dozen PTEs—none of which he or other officials would identify. In Iowa, Ellen Gordon, the state's homeland security adviser, says "our Department of Public Safety figures there may be three or four terrorist-type cells" in the state, but she declined to identify them.

Monitoring Dissident Groups

Having spurred many states and localities into launching or intensifying programs to monitor dissident groups, Ashcroft's Justice Department is now supporting a series of training programs that explicitly urge police to worry not just about Al Qaeda-style terrorists but also about environmentalists and other troublesome activists. The core program was launched by one of Justice's twenty-eight Regional Community Policing Institutes, based at Wichita State University in Kansas, which helps train police from 650 departments in Kansas and Nebraska. In its curriculum, called *A Police Response to Terrorism in the Heartland: Integrating Law Enforcement Intelligence and Community Policing*, the Wichita institute urges police to collect information on "enemies in our own backyard," including "the Green Movement"—described in a footnote as "environmental activism that is aimed at political and social reform with the explicit attempt to develop environmental-friendly policy, law and behavior."

"We have a virtual buffet of political extremism out here," says David Carter, a professor at the School of Criminal Justice at Michigan State University and one of two authors of the curriculum. Carter, an instructor at the Wichita training site, warns that the police ought to be concerned "not just with Al Qaeda but with the groups involved in the [World Economic Forum] protests in New York, or the World Trade Organization protesters." Sorting out the means to do this without violating the civil liberties of protest groups is tricky, says Carter. "How do we balance—which is a real conundrum—homeland security with our constitutional rights? Which is more important? Are our rights important, if we are being blown up?"

At the Justice Department, Dr. Sandra Webb, an official in the policing institute division, tried to distance herself from Carter's curriculum, asserting that the material used in Wichita reflects only the opinions of the authors. But she did not disassociate the Justice Department from it, and she said that it will be presented to representatives of all twenty-eight institutes so that it can be made available to police departments across the country. "We are trying to make it better known," she says. "There will be a lot of interest."

With polls showing large majorities of Americans willing to sacrifice civil liberties for security, and with Congress competing to outbid Ashcroft and Ridge in the war on terrorism, there is little to restrain the agglomeration of police powers by the FBI and state and local law enforcement. In the past, such restraints have been imposed only when widespread abuses have come to light, often many years after they began, leading to a public outcry. As the permanent war on terrorism unfolds, a decade may pass before the trauma of September 11 wears off and the pendulum begins to swing back—and by then, it's more than likely that Congressional committees and investigative reporters will be unearthing new, cold-war-style abuses.

Freedom vs. Security

Fareed Zakariah

Following the September 11 attacks, the American government took actions designed to ensure the domestic security of the nation. Airport security was tightened, and Congress passed the USA Patriot Act, which gave the FBI expanded powers to conduct wiretapping and surveillance. While most Americans supported these efforts, many raised concerns about their potential to infringe on the civil liberties of citizens. In the following selection, Fareed Zakariah explores the tension between the need to protect citizens' security while also ensuring that their freedom of movement, speech, and due process are maintained. Zakariah is an editor for *Newsweek*.

I will always remember July 4, 2001, because a week earlier I became an American citizen. It was a different America one year ago. The country was bathed in peace and plenty, calmly contemplating a mild recession and a sinking stock market. But underneath the surface, Americans were searching for purpose. You could feel it in the insatiable appetite for tales of American heroes: Tom Brokaw's "Greatest Generation" books, the spate of best sellers about Washington, Jefferson and Adams, the resonance of John McCain's rhetoric. At the time, I thought that we should enjoy the peace and quiet, for it would not last. "You can't manufacture a great cause out of a sense of nostalgia for old ones," I wrote. "When America was threatened, as in World War II and the cold war, it rose to the task. And it will when the next crisis arises."

Well, here we are, one July 4 later. We have our crisis and our cause. We no longer need to read about heroes in history books; we have watched the firefighters and policemen of New York City court death to save strangers. We have heard the stories of the brave men and women of Flight 93. We have seen soldiers in Afghanistan risking their lives to rid us of danger. The United States has risen to the task, though many Americans are now wistful about those piping times of peace. As they should be. War tests a nation's character, but the goal of any civilized nation is to meet the test so as to make new ones unnecessary. John Adams said that he studied war and politics so that his sons could study navigation and commerce, so that their sons could study poetry and music.

For now we are all studying war. But it is a strange kind of war, without a country to fight against, without a conventional military struggle, without even a clear sense of how we will know we have won. The urgency of last fall has given way not to normalcy—we are too often interrupted by crises, warnings and arrests for that—but to uncertainty. No one knows how vast or puny the enemy is or how exactly we should fight him. Most of all, we don't know how to protect ourselves in this vast, free society. It is easy to imagine the worst. The summer blockbusters leave little to the imagination. In "The Sum of All Fears," a Baltimore stadium gets blown up during the Super Bowl by a dirty nuclear bomb. The movies then morph into the nightly news and we hear of the arrest of Jose Padilla, the man suspected of seeking just such a bomb. We watch Steven Spielberg's new movie, "Minority Report," in which a Department of Pre-Crime arrests Americans who are potential criminals. And then we remember that Padilla has been locked up, not for anything he has done that was illegal but for things he might have done—for pre-crimes. As far as we know, about 1,200 men rounded up by the Justice Department since September 11 who are being held—in some cases without bail, formal charges or legal counsel—are all guilty of pre-crimes. And yet, the government must act quickly and on sketchy evidence, or else it will be too late. The president has designated Padilla an "enemy combatant," and what he is suspected of is better thought of not as pre-crime but pre-war.

In that sense, in America's intelligence agencies we have always had departments of pre-war. Only now they must operate at home.

On one matter there seems to be general agreement—September 11 changed everything. The United States has been attacked at home. The danger is ever present. The enemy is within.

But in fact the United States has had to deal with situations much like this one ever since its founding. In the late 1790s the fledgling American republic faced a mortal threat from France, which had launched an undeclared war at sea. In that climate, President John Adams signed the Alien and Sedition Acts, designed to make life difficult for French immigrants and for Adams's great rival, Thomas Jefferson, and his followers, whose pro-French views seemed treasonous in a time of crisis. These acts, parts of which were plainly unconstitutional, paled in comparison to what Abraham Lincoln did during the Civil War. Worried about Confederate saboteurs, Lincoln repeatedly suspended the right of due process. "Lincoln's attitude was, if anyone gives you trouble, arrest him and throw him into jail. It's that simple," says Civil War historian Shelby Foote. Or consider the Red Scare of 1919, which began with a series of terrorist bombings. In June 1919 senior government officials started receiving package bombs. By 1920 more bombs had damaged the facades of the New York Stock Exchange and the Morgan bank. The Justice Department's investigation, headed by the 24-year-old J. Edgar Hoover, capitalized on public fears. It arrested 4,000 people, broke up communist meetings and deported about 400 suspect aliens with little legal process.

The most recent example of dealing with enemies within is, of course, the early 1950s. While Joseph McCarthy's ghoulish tactics were repugnant, we now know from the Soviet archives that the Kremlin did maintain a spy network within the American government. Consider the times. In August 1949 the Soviet Union exploded an atomic bomb. Nuclear weapons were new, and many feared that the ideologues who ran the Kremlin and preached world revolution might use them. Then China, with a quarter of the world's

population, fell to communism. The next year communist
North Korea invaded South Korea. And during this period,
Alger Hiss and Julius and Ethel Rosenberg were caught spy-
ing for the Soviet Union. This climate of fear resulted in
congressional hearings, new laws, blacklists and vastly expanded powers for Hoover's FBI.

It's easy to dismiss that period as an overreaction to a limited threat. Compare it, however, with what we face today.
Al Qaeda is a determined but ragtag bunch of Third World
revolutionaries and nihilists, without a single country in the
world that will openly house, feed and supply them. In the
early 1950s the second most powerful country in the world,
with nuclear weapons and dozens of major allies, was actively seeking to infiltrate America and its government.

We have been here before. America has a long history—
some of it good, some bad—of trying to ensure the security
of its citizens against mortal threats from within. Nothing in
our present crisis suggests that we need throw away that history, those lessons or our fundamental belief that liberty can
indeed be balanced with security. The question is how to do
it this time.

Attorney General John Ashcroft often defends the expansion of his powers by reminding Americans that "we are at
war." And he's right. The government should be given much
leeway to deter and disrupt those who seek to kill Americans.
But the greatest obstacle to fighting terror is not our freedom
but government inefficiency. When the Department of Justice sends out one of its now routine terror alerts, they go to
18,000 law-enforcement agencies around the country. Have
you ever wondered why we have 18,000 law-enforcement
agencies? The crazy-quilt structure of American government, with local, state and federal authority, overlapping
agencies and shared powers, is the single greatest threat to
America's safety.

It's difficult to organize and reorganize government to
meet this new challenge. It's easy to show resolve by round-
ing up foreigners, fingerprinting people and asserting new
powers. Ashcroft has warned against even discussing violations of civil liberties, saying, "To those who scare peace-

loving people with phantoms of lost liberty, my message is this: your tactics only aid terrorists." But who is the greater help to terrorists today, the American Civil Liberties Union or the National Rifle Association? The FBI is finding out all it can about the 1,200 people rounded up since September 11—except whether they have ever bought firearms. It's not that the government doesn't have that information, but the Justice Department will not share it because of an NRA-sponsored law that says that information about people buying guns—even illegal immigrants!—can never be shared with anyone. Ashcroft defends this policy. Perhaps someone should remind him that we are at war.

In a time of national crisis, we must trust the government. But trusting the government is not the same as trusting the executive branch. The USA PATRIOT Act, which gave the government most of its new powers after September 11, has bypassed and undermined the role of the courts in several key areas—eavesdropping, attorney-client privileges. But the founding theory of America is that no one branch should be trusted with exclusive powers. "If men were angels," Madison wrote in the Federalist Papers, "no government would be necessary."

In 1945, as the cold war began, one could have made the case that America needed a much stronger central government. But after a 50-year cold war and the creation of a vast national-security establishment that spends hundreds of billions of dollars a year, it's difficult to argue that the executive branch doesn't have the muscle it needs. (What it needs is smarts.)

This push for unilateral power is the natural impulse of every president. In 1952, in the midst of the Korean War, Harry Truman determined that an upcoming steel strike would cripple America's war effort. He ordered the seizure of the steel mills, using his powers as commander in chief. The Supreme Court ruled, however, that the action was unconstitutional. Not because the government could not nationalize the steel industry. It could. But the executive branch could not do so unilaterally. Even in war, checks and balances were crucial. The conservative legal scholar Ruth

Wedgwood argues that the executive should have to justify its designation of men like Padilla as "enemy combatants" to a panel of judges. Americans should not be arrested simply on John Ashcroft's say-so. This is not because Ashcroft is evil. It is because he is human.

The one area where America—government and people—has vastly improved on its past is in its treatment of a threatened minority during war. From the start, President Bush, New York's Mayor Rudolph Giuliani and almost all other national leaders sounded the call for tolerance and asked Americans not to vent their anger on people who were (or looked like) Arabs. There were many attacks on such people—by some counts, more than 400—but the government has been vigorous in prosecuting the offenders. A district attorney in Indiana told me that in one such case he was pressed by the federal government to ask for the most severe punishment possible to send a signal that such behavior was unacceptable. Considering the nature of the September 11 attacks and the size of this country, we should be proud that for the most part America lived up to its ideals.

One thing bothers some Americans: the airport searches. I have heard commentator after commentator angrily wonder why 80-year-old white women are being thoroughly searched while swarthy young men with exotic names walk freely onboard. "Stop those men," they thunder. Relax. As a swarthy young man with an exotic name, trust me, we're being checked. I don't know what the system is and how much discretion is allowed the security guards at the gates, but I've taken more than 50 flights all over the country since September 11, and I've been searched about 60 percent of the time. Either they are checking me out or I'm the unluckiest man alive.

What's more, I don't object to it. At least not on ethical grounds. If the pool of suspects is overwhelmingly of a particular ethnic/racial/religious group, then it only makes sense to pay greater attention to people of that background. But were this one factor to trigger a search, I'd be opposed, not on moral grounds but because it's stupid. Here the homeland-security crowd could learn something from local police. Racial profiling is less and less used by police departments, and not because it's increasingly being outlawed but rather because it doesn't work.

It's not that there isn't a racial profile that one could compose. After all, in most major American cities, young black and Latino men are still overwhelmingly the most likely perpetrators of many kinds of crime. But police forces have found that racial profiling doesn't work. David Harris, an authority on racial profiling who has interviewed hundreds of cops, explains that race is too broad a category to be useful. "Every cop will tell you what's important is suspicious behavior," Harris says. "If you focus on race, the eye is distracted from behavior and moves to what is literally skin deep." Customs Service agents have also learned this lesson. They used to stop blacks and Latinos at vastly disproportionate rates to whites. Then they switched and began using information and behavior as their criteria. They looked at where and how tickets were bought, did background checks, watched whether you stuck to your bags at all times. As a result, they searched fewer people and found twice as many blacks and whites, and five times as many Latinos, who were running drugs.

The key to the information revolution is that good information, properly used, is the most effective weapon any organization can have. Vincent Cannistraro, former head of counterterrorism at the CIA, explains that racial profiling is bad information. "It's a false lead. It may be intuitive to stereotype people, but profiling is too crude to be effective. I can't think of any examples where profiling has caught a terrorist." With this particular enemy, racial profiling would be pointless. Consider the four most famous accused terrorists in custody today: John Walker Lindh, a white American; Zacarias Moussaoui, an African with a French passport; Richard Reid, a half-West Indian, half-Englishman with a British passport; Jose Padilla, a Hispanic American. They are all Muslim, but that broadens the category to the point of uselessness. There are 1.2 billion Muslims in the world, and even in the United States there are several million. "If you're looking for a needle in a haystack, adding hay isn't going to help," says the Arab-American activist James Zogby.

What we need is not profiling but smart profiling. Stephen Flynn of the Council on Foreign Relations is among the leading homeland-security experts in the country. Flynn argues that you start with reverse profiling. People who are low risk should be "precleared." When you buy your ticket, the airline asks the FBI to run your name through its database. If you come out clean, you go through a "green line." That way the inspections process can focus on the much smaller group of people about whom the government has either suspicions or too little information—the "red line." (Every one of the September 11 hijackers would have had to go through such a red line had it been in place.) "That narrows the field," says Flynn, "not in a dumb way as race or religion would, but in a smart way." Flynn argues that above all else, interrogation and intuition are what works. "The Feds need to be able to observe and talk to the small number of suspicious people rather than doing broad or random searches," he says. "Behavior is usually the giveaway, in terrorism as in crime."

Overly broad, ethnically based profiling has one other practical problem. It hurts the government's ability to form good relations with these groups, get information and recruit double agents. If there are Qaeda sympathizers within the American Arab or Muslim communities—and there surely are—the best way to find out is to gain allies within the communities. That's why Cannistraro believes the FBI's decision to round up 5,000 Arabs for questioning is "counterproductive. It alienates the very community whose cooperation you need to get good intelligence." And consider how some of these interrogations take place. An Arab artist living in Brooklyn—who asked that his name be withheld—was taken in for questioning by two FBI agents. He was put in a lower-Manhattan cell where guards told him to shut up and an FBI agent muttered, "They'll let any of you sorry motherf—-ers in this country now?" Two agents interrogated him for three hours and then threw him in jail for the night. After being given a Snickers bar for dinner, he slept on a concrete floor with two other Arab-immigrant men. In the morning they informed him that they now "liked him," and asked if he would like to join the FBI's fight against terrorism and help translate during other interviews such as the one he went through. Guess what: he declined.

Unlike many European countries where immigrants live a bitter, resentful life outside the mainstream, in America new minorities have tended to integrate into the broader community. There are doubtless elements within Muslim or Arab communities here that are sympathetic to Al Qaeda. But finding out who they are requires gaining the trust of the vast majority who are in America because they want the American dream.

In 1942, eight Nazi agents—all German-Americans or Germans who had lived in the United States for long stretches—landed on New York's Long Island with instructions to destroy American power plants, factories and bridges. They were captured by the FBI, President Roosevelt declared them enemy combatants and they were tried and convicted by a military tribunal. This case—Ex parte Quirin—is the model often cited to explain how we should fight the war on terror bluntly and robustly. But it leaves out one part of the story. The FBI had no idea that these men had landed and knew nothing of their plans. The terrorists were discovered only because one of the eight men was an American patriot. He had set off on the mission with the intention of divulging the plot to the authorities. America must change a great deal as it fights this new and strange war on terror. But let us ensure it always remains the kind of country for which people will make such sacrifices.

Chapter 4

The Next Phase: How Should the War Proceed?

Turning | Points

IN WORLD HISTORY

The War on Terrorism Will Require a Lighter, More Agile Military

Jason Vest

Jason Vest is a Washington-based senior correspondent for the *American Prospect*. In the following article, Vest describes some of the tactics and strategies that military leaders think will be necessary to counter terrorists. He contends that the military must prepare for "fourth-generation" warfare. Such warfare is characterized by "asymmetric" operations, in which one side undermatches the other in power and therefore bypasses military targets and instead strikes directly at cultural, political, or civilian targets. In order to respond to this type of warfare, the author argues, America needs a decentralized military consisting of small, fast-moving units with light equipment.

Pentagon mavericks have been trying for decades to reorient military strategy toward a new kind of threat—the kind we're suddenly facing in the war on terrorism. Now that we've got the war they predicted, will we get the reforms they've been pushing for?

For all the tactical twists and turns in U.S. military planning during and since the Cold War, the basic strategic template has remained more or less the same. To simplify mightily, the emphasis has been on a doctrine of attrition [destroying enemy equipment and soldiers] and theater warfare against large, identifiable foes with professional standing armies. This strategy has gone hand in hand with an emphasis on costly high-tech weapons systems designed to project force from a distance. Some of these weapons sys-

Jason Vest, "Fourth Generation Warfare," *Atlantic Monthly*, vol. 288, December 2001, pp. 48–50. Copyright © 2001 by Atlantic Monthly. Reproduced by permission of the author.

tems are dubious, and the procurement system as a whole is characterized by cronyism, turf battles, and waste. To be sure, not everything about the traditional outlook is bad, and the American military is in important respects without parallel. It is capable of a crushing global reach, which in certain circumstances can destroy opposing forces with limited risk. But the U.S. military also has trouble reacting quickly, and it has tended to think far more about the kinds of battles we won't be fighting than about the real-world conflicts we're about to be embroiled in.

The terrorist attacks on the United States in September 2001, orchestrated by the Osama bin Laden organization, have now placed the issue of the military's orientation plainly in the public view. In one corner stand advocates for something along the lines of the status quo (whatever they may now say about the need for "flexibility"). In the opposing corner are champions of the late John Boyd, a colonel in the Air Force and an innovative theorist who considered that large, expensive weapons systems that took forever to produce were as much of an enemy as hostile foreign powers. . . . Boyd advocated reforms—many of which have been successfully adopted by the Marine Corps but have met with resistance elsewhere, particularly in the Army—that stressed a number of inter-related elements. Chief among them: adaptability and agility as the driving forces of combat; weapons that are dependable, simple, and cheap; and decentralization of command and communications, so that fighting units aren't at the mercy of layers of decision-makers.

The inheritor of Boyd's mantle is a Pentagon weapons analyst named Franklin C. "Chuck" Spinney, who has spent the past two decades arguing that static thinking, poor financial oversight, weapons-procurement bloat, and a personnel system that accentuates careerism over training have undermined America's war-fighting readiness. (For anyone interested in these topics, Spinney's Web site, Defense and the National Interest—www.d-n-i.net—is indispensable.) As Spinney sees it, the September 11 attacks call attention to something that a number of military reformers have been warning about for years: the advent of "fourth-generation warfare" [4GW], and the fact that the U.S. military isn't ready for it. As Spinney observed on his Web site recently, the attacks on the Pentagon and the World Trade Center have "dispelled forever the notion that 4GW is just 'terrorism' or something that happens only in poverty-stricken Third World countries."

In the Boydian view, first-generation warfare was defined by close-order formations armed with guns to repel sword-and-bayonet cavalry and infantry, something the young Napoleon perfected. Second-generation warfare's winners were those who had the most, or the best-managed, firepower, enabling their forces to win through attrition—an approach mastered by the Prussian army. Third-generation warfare saw second-generation armies being agitated by decentralized attacks that, though brilliant, ultimately failed by virtue of an opponent's ability to wear the attacker down. An example would be the Ludendorff offensives of 1918, when an initially successful German drive against the Allies ultimately stalled.

American Military Strategy Stuck in the Past

In their essay "Why It Is Time to Adapt to Changing Conditions," Spinney, Army Major Donald Vandergriff, and Marine Lieutenant Colonel John Sayen observe that even though the Cold War is over, American military doctrine is still firmly rooted in second-generation thinking, which better serves a largely politicized high command, Congress, and defense contractors than it does national security. In their view, the Clinton and Bush Administrations and the military establishment have been keeping alive defense projects that might have had some utility in a bygone era, while paying only lip service to doctrine and weapons for fourth-generation warfare.

Viewed in the context of military history, fourth-generation warfare is highly irregular. "Asymmetric" operations—in which a vast mismatch exists between the resources and philosophies of the combatants, and in which the emphasis is on bypassing an opposing military force and striking directly at cultural, political, or population targets—are a defining characteristic of fourth-generation warfare. The United States will face decentralized, non-state actors (perhaps supported by a rogue nation or two) who understand just how big an impact attacks on markets, communications, and cultural icons can have on the American psyche. Spinney and his co-authors write of the sorts of enemies that confront us in fourth-generation warfare,

> They usually present few, if any, important targets vulnerable to conventional attack, and their followers are usually much more willing to fight and die for their causes. They seldom wear uniforms and may be difficult to distinguish from the general population. They are also far less hampered by convention and more likely to seek new and innovative means to achieve their objectives.

Fourth-Generation Warfare Involves Politics, Diplomacy, and Economics

An enemy who employs 4GW [fourth-generation warfare] tactics views whatever action he takes as one prong of a sustained campaign in the service of a political objective (and a political objective, despite all the focus on the bin Laden organization's religious zeal, is something bin Laden has). Contrary to advocates of standard U.S. military thinking, American proponents of 4GW see the role of the armed forces when confronted with this kind of situation as crucial but also of limited prominence—the military mission is tied closely to diplomatic, political, and economic initiatives that focus on eroding the enemy's popular support. "Perhaps most odd of all," Spinney has written on his Web site, "being seen as 'too successful' militarily may create a backlash, making the opponent's other elements of 4GW more effective."

As Spinney, Vandergriff, and Sayen observe, ever since the end of the Cold War the Pentagon has lagged in developing the correct military response to 4GW—a response that calls for reliance on smaller units versed in maneuver warfare. This kind of fighting eschews heavy firepower, attrition, and longrange, high-altitude bombardment. It favors joint-service operations and close-quarters combat involving small, fast-moving units with lighter equipment.

Under the leadership of Commandants Alfred Gray and

Charles Krulak, the Marine Corps began implementing these ideas even before the Cold War ended. In 1999, when General Eric Shinseki became the Army's chief of staff, he made it clear that he, too, was a maneuver-warfare advocate, and stated that he wanted to be able to deploy a new, streamlined, medium-sized combat brigade anywhere in the world within ninety-six hours. Although many junior and midlevel officers were buoyed by Shinseki's ambitions, they have been disappointed by how little headway he has in fact made. One big obstacle: entrenched senior subordinates who are simply resistant to change. "Other chiefs of staff have tried to do this sort of thing," says one Army officer not enamored of his time at the Pentagon, "and like them, Shinseki has essentially been undermined by colonels who are more bureaucrats than warriors." Who the soldier bureaucrats are—and how they got where they are and manage to stay there—is of particular interest to Donald Vandergriff, who has made an extensive study of the Army's personnel system and believes that now is the time to undertake a program of genuine reform. At the moment, he points out, the system isn't set up for optimal results against the kind of enemy the Boydians think is most likely to threaten America—the kind that attacked us on September 11. "This is not a war where you're going to fight a formation of opposing units," Vandergriff says. "And if you were really serious about acknowledging and addressing the reality of fourth-generation warfare, you would work hard to get and keep quality people in the military, and keep captains and NCOs [non-commissioned officers] and their units together longer so they have more cohesion and can train more effectively. We could also start by cutting the size of the officer corps—do we really need three hundred and eighty-six generals in the Army, each with a staff that generates its own paperwork? The current personnel system is in the industrial age and is at the heart of what's wrong with the system today."

And then there's the accounting system. Even though Defense Department auditors and congressional investigators have found that over the past five years the armed services couldn't account for tens of billions of dollars, no one has taken steps to change what amounts to standard operating procedure. If any other agency of the government failed, according to its own auditors, to account satisfactorily for such large amounts of money, an overhaul would be swift in coming.

In theory this is something that the 1997 Quadrennial Defense Review—and its 2001 successor, which was delivered to Congress in September—should have addressed. Neither review did so. Spinney had proposed a one-year freeze on all budget programs, followed by a real effort to "get the Pentagon to think before it spends." This hasn't really happened. Although hastily rewritten to emphasize a commitment to "homeland defense" over missile defense, the most recent QDR is short on specifics and indefinitely postpones crucial decisions, notably on items such as personnel and procurement. It does keep three major fighter-aircraft projects alive—a victory for 2GW.

Congress Must Act to Reform Military

The possibility of a revolutionary overhaul of the military has grown remote. "The September 11 attacks," Spinney says, "which cost the perpetrators all of five-hundred thousand dollars, don't justify an increase in the defense budget—we're spending as much on defense already as the next fifteen countries do combined. Look at where the new money is going to go—it purports to help us deal with this problem, but it's going to fund all the other crap." Spinney says he won't be surprised if the money ends up getting used to buy more F-22s for the Air Force, more self-propelled Crusader howitzers for the Army, and more submarines for the Navy.

There is, however, an idea from World War II that is worth revisiting—one that both President Franklin D. Roosevelt and the military leadership saw as eminently patriotic and also crucial to winning the war: Senator Harry S. Truman's Special Committee to Investigate the National Defense Program. The committee's official mandate was to "investigate all activities" involving national defense; Truman himself described the job as being "to dig this stuff up now and correct it": and the Truman Committee ended up saving American taxpayers hundreds of millions of dollars. Today, with $40 billion earmarked for a major war against terror-ism, many of those interviewed for this article argue that Congress must play a specific oversight role to ensure that the money is spent wisely and properly. This isn't something that should be left to any of the standing armed-services committees, which are compromised by longtime ties to de-fense contractors and the military bureaucracy. The job must fall to some new entity in Congress—something as new as the threats we now confront.

A Long-Term Strategy Is Needed in the War on Terrorism

Charles L. Armstrong

Charles L. Armstrong was a career infantry officer in the U.S. Marines. He retired after twenty-five years of combined enlisted and commissioned service, during which he served in four shooting wars.

In the following article, Armstrong outlines his proposal for how the war on terrorism should be conducted. In the short-term, he calls for retaliation against those responsible for the attacks of September 11, retribution for the victims, and financial contributions from nations that are not willing to provide military support to the campaign. He especially emphasizes the need to prepare for the long-term nature of the struggle, which he likens to a counterinsurgency. More specifically, he recommends changing laws to make it easier to conduct intelligence gathering and counterterrorism efforts abroad, calling up retired military personnel, and mandatory military service. In addition, he argues that America must reduce its dependence on foreign oil and shore up the security of its communications and infrastructure.

When the Washington lawmakers finish fleshing out the Bush doctrine, it will read something like this: 'America will make no distinction between those who carry out terrorist attacks on the United States and its citizens, and those individuals, governments, or factions which give them safe harbor, sanctuary, or support.'

Throughout the history of our country, various Presi-

Charles L. Armstrong, "The Bush Doctrine and the War on Terrorism," *Marine Corps Gazette*, vol. 85, November 2001, pp. 76–79. Copyright © 2001 by Marine Corps Association. Reproduced by permission.

dents have implied the same thing—Monroe, for example, with his mandate to protect the Americas from European incursion, and Teddy Roosevelt, with his challenge to North African brigands ("America wants Perdicarious alive, or the Raissouli dead!").

President Bush's bold statement and his virtual declaration of war on terrorism have the same flavor of American hyperbole but carry different connotations than the war cries of yesteryear. In the article that follows, I offer a framework for executing the Bush doctrine, point out pitfalls, and provide potential solutions for problems our Nation faces vis-a-vis the doctrine as I see it developing.

Retaliation, Retribution, Contribution, and Long-Term Solution

The course upon which our Nation has embarked in the wake of vicious attacks against our financial capital and the brain trust of the world's greatest military is tough to argue. As our President said, "We will smoke these people out and bring them to justice . . . dead or alive . . ." Clearly, the faction that executed the attacks of 11 September committed an act of war against our country on par with the Japanese attack against Pearl Harbor in 1941. However, the mechanics of answering this attack with a formal declaration of war are difficult.

A nation-state cannot declare war against a nameless piece of real estate, nor should we declare war against an individual, faction, or faceless "evil." What we should do—and what our President appears to be doing—is declare a long-term physical campaign against philosophical forces determined to alter our way of life.

I see the campaign in four phases: retaliation, retribution, contribution, and long-term solution.

This first, ruthless stage of the campaign [retaliation] needs to come soon, be executed against the clearest possible suspects in the attacks against our country's infrastructure, and be visible to the world community. America and her allies will accept this retaliatory action, if it is launched soon and publicly. The longer we wait, the more we'll be subjected to Monday morning quarterbacking at home and abroad. For a few more days, the world will accept "overkill."

The next phase in the campaign is retribution. Through a combination of diplomatic and economic endeavors, we should encourage other countries to stand beside us for the longer haul in the war against global terrorism. As we do this we should squeeze the financial resources of individuals, factions, or nations that have sponsored terrorist groups, both as a means of financing the war and paying for cleanup at home. When the world operated on gold bullion, this would have been problematic. Today, with electronic transfers of money, it is relatively simple.

As an example, the Governor of New York has announced a program to provide college tuition to children of people killed in the World Trade Center (WTC) attack. Although this is commendable leadership by Governor Pataki, I would prefer to see a terrorist organization or a sponsoring country foot that bill.

The airline industry has asked for emergency funding of $24 billion in the wake of September's disaster. I think exacting this tribute from appropriate foreign entities would be pretty neat.

If we conduct a detailed postmortem of financial transactions that provided direct enrichment to people, companies, or consortia that could not have reasonably assumed a catastrophe of this magnitude was imminent, we'll be on the scent of dirty money. Following the money will permit us to appropriate the right bank or brokerage accounts and put a few more names on the target lists.

This leads us to contribution. Although many nations have offered condolences and support to America, there are some conditions laid out in the fine print. Japan, for instance, has stated it can offer no military support because of its constitution. Pakistan is trying to be a good neighbor but hinted early it would like U.S. support for debt relief to the tune of $30 billion. Some countries will encourage its citizens to give blood, as long as it's not on the battlefield and so forth.

That's all OK. Nobody ever said playing the role of the world's single superpower would be easy, and Americans have for generations been accustomed to leading the way among freedom-loving nations.

I believe we should levy a war tax, however, against those international partners who cannot step up to the war on terrorism with troops. This is akin to political and emotional blackmail (think of all the guilt mail you got recently that started with, "Are you against child abuse and drugs in our schools?") but is a rational way to take the fight forward without troops from countries whose national psyche may not be up to "smokin' 'em out."

Long-Term Solution

This is the tough one. Like it or not, we're a Nation of short-term solutions. Our stock market fluctuations are a function of quarterly earnings reports, news of which we start to leak a month in advance of quarterly close. With the advent of online trading and CNBC, we can watch short-term fluctuations driven by news releases several times an hour. We change fashions seasonally, year after year. With the demise of stable corporations offering employment for life in exchange for loyalty, we change jobs more frequently than we change addresses. This isn't criticism, merely commentary on a culture of the short-term view.

Funding and staffing the war on terrorism will be hard, particularly with respect to long-term political will. It is one thing to gather unequivocal support for a massive military strike against terrorist strongholds executed in days, with little direct impact on the folks back home. It is something else to think of a "long campaign" (to use the term President Bush employed during an interview with French President Chirac on 18 September, and reiterated by Secretary of State Colin Powell a day later). To visualize such a campaign, one must think of a military counterinsurgency.

Veterans of such campaigns know counterinsurgencies try the national patience, while draining the national manpower of blood and the national treasury of money. We fought a 25-year counterinsurgency in Southeast Asia, for example, and lost. The experience divided the Nation like no other episode since the War Between the States. Colombia has been fighting the same war for nearly 50 years with no end in sight. In the Congo the same war has been raging since 1960, featuring some of the same players. The war in Angola has been running about 25 years.

Millions of Americans have been swept up in patriotic fervor following the attacks on our country. This is right and wonderful, and I am proud to see my countrymen from so many diverse backgrounds come so resolutely together. The Armed Forces Reservists called to active duty will, I believe, serve with distinction and pride. But the day in the campaign will come when tours of duty are up, the tax burden is more than America wants to bear, and we all realize civil liberties we relinquish today are almost impossible to recover tomorrow. What then?

We should prepare for "what then" in advance, even before we make the first strike against the terrorists who had the temerity to challenge our way of life. I encourage a full review of the laws (domestic and international) that govern the use of intrusion and force with respect to combating global banditry and terrorism.

We should reexamine the series of policies that have weakened our ability to conduct human intelligence activities. Unless I'm mistaken, our intelligence services are forbidden to employ resources suspected of human rights violations and other crimes. Just as my boyhood preacher taught that sinners, not the righteous, make up a church's congregation, we should remind ourselves that people who are willing to betray their causes—that is, spy for a foreign power—are rarely altar boys but generally act for money. We should act accordingly and recruit the types of individuals who can successfully engage the terrorist mastermind.

Next, we should look beyond the 2-year horizon implied by the current Reserve Gallup. Our Reserve and National Guard forces are already stretched by peacekeeping and will be further taxed by defending our homeland during the coming campaign. We need a plan to replace those forces, while simultaneously replenishing the Active forces for a potentially prolonged war.

I propose a plan for phased release of Reserve forces,

based on their replacement by recalling to active duty retired members of the Regular military establishment. Such members should be able to meet the rigors of home defense (and I suspect many retired Marines, Airborne Rangers, and Navy SEALs could deploy with relative ease alongside their active duty counterparts). Some skills atrophy and the laws of time affect certain reflexes (those needed by fighter pilots, for instance), but for most skills a sensible rotation plan could be developed in days.

Finally, we need to test the Nation's resolve for the long haul.

"Draft" Is Not a Four-Letter Word

In the hectic days that followed the bombing of Pearl Harbor, thousands of Americans stormed the recruiting stations to enlist in the coming war. Even with a serious economic downturn, I'm not certain the current turnout to fight terrorists has been so robust. The anger of the moment may temporarily swell our active duty ranks, but I'll be surprised if we are still wait-listing people who want to enlist at this time next year [2002]. This is no indictment of American youth or patriotism. It's just that an entire generation of Americans has come of age during a time when military service is neither required nor especially valued.

Recent news stories have mentioned the increasing number of Armed Forces deserters and the absence of censure these deserters face in the civilian workforce or on the homefront. A couple of years ago, the Army was offering a $20,000 signing bonus for infantry enlistees, or about what graduates from good master's of business administration programs could expect. Military recruiters sweat blood to make quotas, and we probably have no real idea what it actually costs to recruit and maintain the all-volunteer force. Again, this isn't an indictment of how we do business, but a framing of the facts as they pertain to our current problem.

We'll know America is serious with respect to fighting and winning the war on terrorism when Congress makes military service mandatory, with exemptions granted solely for mental or physical incompetence. This would accomplish several things. It would underscore our national resolve for the long fight that the war on global terrorism is likely to be. It would make the country stronger. (Do any of us really believe there exists a more resolute fighter—in a battle for the home-land—than the citizen-soldier?) And it would enable us to build and maintain a tough, capable Armed Forces for a much lower pricetag than the cost of the pure, all-volunteer (read, non-draft motivated) force we've had since the early 1970s. That would free up scarce funds for other uses.

Fighting on Nonmilitary Fronts

This kind of war is not won solely on military battlefields. As a Nation we remain too dependent on petroleum imports to have true freedom of action. Without a market-based, long-term plan to reduce our dependence on foreign oil, we (or our allies, or both) will be potentially hostage to a future squeeze. The time to get aggressively creative was 30 years ago, the first time OPEC (Organization of Petroleum Exporting Countries) flexed its muscles. It's not too late, but even with the recent assurances of solidarity from oil-rich friends, it's certainly time.

Despite crowded phone lines and chaos in the streets of New York after the World Trade Center bombings, the Internet functioned with nary a hiccup after the strikes. A few days later, however, the "Nimda" virus was described as the most serious threat to date against the web. We can live through the inconvenience of delayed, routine e-mail, but thousands of critical business uses of the Internet are just that—business critical. Hearty as it is, the Internet is too vulnerable to attack from professional and amateur hackers alike. That has to change.

Within a few days of the attacks on our homeland, acts of violence against people of Middle Eastern origin or Islamic faith cropped up across the map. Most Americans of my generation still view the internment of Japanese Americans during World War II as practically unbelievable, yet it happened in the aftermath of Pearl Harbor. Virtually every Marine who has served abroad has friends from a variety of religious and cultural backgrounds. As a subset of America, we are likely to be tolerant and understanding of cultural differences because of our experiences. However, the dark shadow of genocide (against our own Native Americans) and racial intolerance still haunts our history. Throughout the coming war on terrorism, it will take a conscious, consistent effort to remind all concerned that no one in our society is guilty by association because of national origin or religion.

Finally, we need a different viewpoint with regard to security for what were previously mundane, essentially invisible chunks of vital infrastructure. At least for now we'll live though a period in which every oil refinery, power generation station, brokerage house, sports arena, shopping mall, and elementary school are potential targets. We will have to devise adequate—not failsafe—security measures for our country's infrastructure and revise the way we guard our porous borders.

Thanks to information technology, we can create sophisticated surveillance and response techniques that would have been impossible a few years ago. We can distribute redundant data and communications sites in ways that have thus far been largely experimental or needlessly extravagant. There will be a cost associated with this, but business and (with diplomatic skill and a bit of luck) "contributors" will bear part of it.

What we should not do is impose such crushing restrictions on civil liberties that we dramatically alter the American way of life. If we do that, or if we become so security conscious that we impose too many self-inflicted limitations on how we live, the terrorists who hate us will "win."

Home of the Brave

We have lived through one of those rare, defining moments in American history. None of us will have to think twice to remember exactly what we were doing when we heard about the attacks on New York and Washington. We will all have flashes of perfect, 20/20 hindsight and be tempted to fix blame. . . .

We can't let this pass; we can't be satisfied with a token response; we can't assume a return to business as usual anytime soon. I'm sure other *Marine Corps Gazette* writers who are much closer to the action will send similar views, and Americans will reach that consensus as this drama unfolds.

I expect loud cheers and near-universal approval when we make the first strike in retaliation. The ultimate success of the Bush doctrine will depend on how well we hold together for the long haul and how willing we are as a Nation to share the inevitable sacrifices required for the long campaign. Our former Commandant, [top commander of The Marine Corps] Gen. P.X. Kelley, speaking after a similar tragedy in Lebanon nearly 20 years ago, summed it up pretty well: "If America is to remain the land of the free, we must, in fact, be the home of the brave."

Time will tell if we are brave enough to turn the tough language of the Bush doctrine into a blueprint for a more secure America.

The War on Terror Must Target Militant Islam

Daniel Pipes

Daniel Pipes is director of the Middle East Forum and a columnist for both the *New York Post* and the *Jerusalem Post*. In the following selection, Pipes claims that America's enemy is not "terrorism," but militant Islamic fundamentalism. Terrorism is an abstract concept while militant Islamicists are a concrete enemy with an explicit anti-American program. Pipes describes militant Islam as being composed of three groups: a violent "inner circle," passive believers who sympathize with the militants' vision of an Islamic society, and people who do not believe in the Islamicists' vision but who do share their anti-American sentiments. To defeat militant Islam, the United States must weaken militant Islamic regimes while appealing to the majority of Muslims who are neither violent nor anti-American.

Who is the enemy? The message of September 11 was loud and clear, allowing for no ambiguity: the enemy is militant Islam. No wonder, then, that even before knowing who exactly was responsible, the government has been reluctant to say so. There was the precedent of recent history to deter it.

In February 1995, at the peak of the horrific violence in Algeria that pitted armed and brutal Islamist groups against a repressive government, NATO [North Atlantic Treaty Organization] Secretary General Willy Claes declared that, since the end of the cold war, "Islamic militancy has emerged as perhaps the single gravest threat to the NATO alliance and to Western security." Indeed, Claes said, not

Daniel Pipes, "Who Is the Enemy?" *Commentary*, vol. 113, January 2002, pp. 21–27.

only did militant Islam pose the same kind of threat to the West as Communism before it, but the scale of the danger was greater, for militant Islam encompassed elements of "terrorism, religious fanaticism, and the exploitation of social and economic injustice."

Claes was absolutely correct. But his statements met with outrage from all over the Muslim world, and he was quickly forced to retract and to withdraw. "Religious fundamentalism," he explained lamely, "whether Islamic or of other varieties, is not a concern for NATO."

In the wake of September 11, it may be somewhat easier to say what Claes was not allowed to say then; but only somewhat, and not for anyone in a position of authority. Certain it is that no one wants to have to retrace Claes's red-faced retreat. And yet, awkward as it may be to say, there is no getting around the fact.

Enemy Number One

At least since 1979, when Ayatollah Khomeini [a radical Islamic leader] seized power in Iran with the war-cry, "Death to America," militant Islam, also known as Islamism, has been the self-declared enemy of the United States. It has now become enemy number one. Whether it is the terrorist organizations and individuals Washington is targeting, the immigrants it is questioning, or the states it is holding under suspicion, virtually all are Islamist or connected with Islamists. Washington may not speak its mind, but its actions express its real views.

I want to be clear. To define militant Islam as the country's most worrisome, long-term opponent is hardly to deny the existence of other opponents. There is no single danger as terrifying as Saddam Hussein with nuclear weapons. Nor is there any dearth of other non-Islamic adversaries around the globe, whether within the Muslim orbit (Syria, Libya, the PA [Palestinian Authority]) or outside it (North Korea, Cuba, etc.). But these adversaries lack several features that make militant Islam so threatening—its ideological fervency, its reach, its ambitiousness, and its staying power. However great the Iraqi threat, it is limited to the military dimension, to one odious dictator and his circle, and to raw intimidation. Although the constituency of militant Islam is limited to Muslims, this constituency represents, after all, about a sixth of the human race, enjoys a very high birth rate, and is found in nearly every part of the world.

At a moment when the European-derived extremes of the Communist Left and fascist Right are tired and on the whole ineffectual, militant Islam has proved itself to be the only truly vital totalitarian movement in the world today. As one after another of its leaders has made clear, it regards itself as the only rival, and the inevitable successor, to Western civilization. Although a number of (wrongheaded) Western observers have declared it to be a dying creed, it is likely to remain a force to contend with for years if not for long decades to come.

A Picture of Militant Islam

Let me try to specify with greater exactness the constituency for militant Islam. It is divisible into three main elements.

The first is the inner core, made up of the likes of Osama bin Laden, the nineteen hijackers, al Qaeda [Osama bin Laden's terrorist group], leaders of the Taliban regime in Afghanistan, and the rest of the network of violent groups inspired by militant Islamic ideology. Such groups have mostly come into existence since 1970, becoming since then a more and more important force in the Muslim world. The network, dubbed the "Islamintern" [from commintern, the old international communist organization] by some Muslim critics, contains both Shiite and Sunni variants, appeals to rich and poor alike, and is active in such far-flung locations as Afghanistan, Algeria, and Argentina. In 1983 some of its members initiated a campaign of violence against the United States whose greatest triumph so far was the spectacular operation on September 11. In all, the network's adherents are as few as they are fanatical, numbering perhaps in the thousands.

The second ring comprises a much larger population of militants who are sympathetic to al Qaeda's radical utopian vision without themselves being a part of it. Their views were on display daily as soon as hostilities began in Afghanistan: protesters and mujahideen by the tens of thousands, all expressing a determined loathing of the United States and an enthusiasm for further acts of violence.

Countries not normally heard from, and hardly hotbeds of radicalism, came to life to protest the U.S. campaign.

The chants of these Islamists across the world bore a certain family resemblance:

Indonesia: "U.S., Go to Hell!"

Malaysia: "Go To Hell America" and "Destroy America."

Bangladesh: "Death to America" and "Osama is our hero."

India: "Death to America. Death to Israel. Taliban, Taliban, we salute you."

Sri Lanka: "Bin Laden we are with you."

Oman: "America is the enemy of God."

Yemen: "America is a great Satan."

Egypt: "U.S. go to hell, Afghans will prevail."

Sudan: "Down, down USA!"

Bosnia: "Long live bin Laden."

United Kingdom: "Tony Blair burn in hell."

As best I can estimate from election data, survey research, anecdotal evidence, and the opinions of informed observers, this Islamist element constitutes some 10 to 15 percent of the total Muslim world population of roughly one billion— that is, some 100 to 150 million persons worldwide.

The third ring consists of Muslims who do not accept the militant Islamic program in all its particulars but do concur with its rank anti-Americanism. This sentiment is found at almost every point along the political spectrum. A secular fascist like Saddam Hussein shares a hatred of the United States with the far leftists of the PKK Kurdish group [Kurdish Workers Party—a group fighting for independence for the Kurdish people in Turkey], who in turn share it with an eccentric figure like [Libyan leader] Muammar Qaddafi. Reliable statistics on opinion in the Muslim world do not exist, but my sense is that one half of the world's Muslims—or some 500 million persons—sympathize more with Osama bin Laden and the Taliban than with the United States. That such a vast multitude hates the United States is sobering indeed.

That is not to say, of course, that anti-Americanism is universal among Muslims, for important bastions of pro-American sentiment do exist. These include the officer corps of the Turkish military, who are the final arbiters of their country's destiny; several leaders of Muslim-majority states in the former Soviet Union; the emerging dissident element in the Islamic Republic of Iran; and, more generally, those Muslims who have experienced at first hand the dominion of militant Islam.

But these constitute a minority. Elsewhere, and everywhere, anti-Americanism rears its head: among the sheltered females of the Saudi elite and the male denizens of Cairo's vast slums, among the aged in remote reaches of Pakistan, and among the students at a Muslim school in the suburbs of Washington, D.C. Nor is hostility always limited to feelings. Since Vietnam, and even before September 11, more Americans died at the hands of Muslim radicals than from any other enemy.

The situation, then, is grim. But it is not hopeless, any more than the situation at the height of the cold war with the Soviet Union was hopeless. What is required, now as then, is not just precision and honesty in defining the enemy but conceptual clarity in confronting it. And perhaps the first step toward that end is to understand that, paradoxical as it may seem in the light of the statistics I have presented above, Americans are not involved in a battle royal between Islam and the West, or what has been called a "clash of civilizations."

This famous term was first given wide currency by the political scientist Samuel Huntington. It has been seconded, in his own diabolical way, by Osama bin Laden. The idea exercises an undoubted appeal, but it happens not to be accurate. True, many Islamist elements do seek such a confrontation, out of a conviction that Islam will prevail and go on to achieve global supremacy. But several facts militate against so sweeping a view of the objective situation.

Diversity Within Islam

For one thing, violence against Americans—and against Israelis, Westerners, and non-Muslims in general—is just part of the story; Islamist enmity toward Muslims who do not share the Islamist outlook is no less vicious. Did not the Taliban reign in Afghanistan make this clear? Their multiple atrocities and gratuitous acts of cruelty toward their fellow Muslims suggested an attitude that bordered on the genocidal; what it felt like to be liberated from that repressive cruelty was well captured in a *New York Times* report from a town in Afghanistan on November 13:

> In the twelve hours since the Taliban soldiers left this town, a joyous mood has spread. The people of Taliqan, who lived for two years under the Taliban's oppressive Islamic rule, burst onto the streets to toss off the restrictions that had burrowed into the most intimate aspects of their lives. Men tossed their turbans into the gutters. Families dug up their longhidden television sets. Restaurants blared music. Cigarettes flared, and young men talked of growing their hair long.

Nor are the Taliban an exception: militant Islam has brutalized Muslims wherever it has achieved power, and wherever it has striven for power. I have already mentioned Algeria, a country that, thanks to a decade of barbarity by Islamists, and with something like 100,000 fatalities and counting, has become a byword for violence against fellow believers. But comparable if smaller-scale orgies of killing have taken place in Egypt, Lebanon, and Turkey. And what can one say of Islamist Iran's war on non-Islamist Iraq after 1982, with its hundreds of thousands of Muslim dead? Militant Islam is an aggressive totalitarian ideology that ultimately discriminates barely if at all among those who stand in its path.

Another reason to question the notion of a clash of civilizations is that it inevitably leads one to ignore important and possibly crucial distinctions within civilizations. Such distinctions emerged with particular poignancy in 1989, when a significant minority of Muslims around the world denounced the death edict issued by Ayatollah Khomeini against the novelist Salman Rushdie—in Iran itself, 127 intellectuals signed a protest against the Khomeini edict— even as more than a few prominent Westerners, secular and religious alike, were apologizing for it or finding some way to "understand" it. (In one typical statement, the president of the French bishops' conference explained that *The Satanic Verses* was an "insult to religion," as though this in some way accounted adequately for the threat on Rushdie's life.)

Or take an example nearer to home and closer in time. After September 11, polls in Catholic Italy found a quarter of Italians holding the view that Americans had gotten what they deserved. Even some Americans sided with the attackers, or at least with their choice of target: "Anyone who can blow up the Pentagon has my vote," announced a professor of history at the University of New Mexico. Does that make these people part of the Muslim world? And what about the tens and hundreds of millions of Muslims who were horrified by the suicide hijackings? Are they not part of the Muslim world?

Islam Need Not Be Militant

This brings us to a large and closely related issue—namely, whether the problem is Islam itself. Like all great religions, Islam is susceptible to a number of interpretations, from the mystical to the militant, from the quietist to the revolutionary. Over a millennium and a half, its most basic ideas have been subjected to highly contrasting explications. That having been said, Islam also differs from other religions in that it includes a large body of regulations about public life that are quite at variance with modern sensibilities and that have not yet been left behind. In short, the hard work of adjusting Islam to the contemporary world has yet really to begin—a fact that itself goes far to explain the attraction of militant Islamic ideology.

That ideology is not an entirely new phenomenon. Its roots go back in some form to the Wahhabi movement of the 18th century, to the writings of Ibn Taymiya in the 13th century, even to the Kharijites of the 7th century. But, as befits a modern-style ideology, today's version covers more aspects of life (including, for example, the economic dimension) than any premodern iteration. It has also enjoyed much greater political success. A radicalized understanding of

Islam has taken hold, possibly over a wider swath than at any other time in the fourteen centuries of Muslim history, and it has driven out or silenced every serious rival.

This radicalism is today's enraged answer to the question that has bedeviled Muslims for 200 years, as the power and wealth that once blessed the world of Islam dribbled away over the five centuries before 1800 and other peoples and nations surged ahead. What went wrong? If Islam brings God's grace, as was widely assumed, why do Muslims fare so poorly? Muslims turned to a number of extremist ideologies in the modern period—from fascism and Leninism to pan-Arabism and pan-Syrianism—all in an attempt to answer that question by almost any means other than introspection, moderation, and self-help. Militant Islam has turned out to be the most popular, the most deluded, and the most disastrous of these ideologies.

But the unprecedented nature of its dominance, ironically, offers hope. However ascendant the militant interpretation may be at present, it need not be so in the future. The terroristic jihad against the West is one reading of Islam, but it is not the eternal essence of Islam. Forty years ago, at the height of the Soviet Union's prestige, and during the heyday of pan-Arab nationalism, militant Islam had scarcely any political influence. What then happened to bring it to the fore is itself a fascinating question, but the point for our purposes is that, just as militant Islam was not a powerful force a scant four decades ago, it is perfectly reasonable to expect that it may not be a powerful force four decades hence.

By contrast, if today's extremism were truly inextricable from Islam, then there would be no solution but to try to quarantine or convert one sixth of humanity. To say the least, neither of those is a realistic prospect.

The Battle for the Soul of Islam

If the earth-shaking clash of our time is not between two civilizations, it is and must be a clash among the members of one civilization—specifically, between Islamists and those who, for want of a better term, we may call moderate Muslims (understanding that "moderate" does not mean liberal or democratic but only anti-Islamist). Just as the deviant Western ideologies of fascism and Communism challenged and shook and had to be expelled from the West, so it is with militant Islam and the Muslim world. The battle for the soul of Islam will undoubtedly last many years and take many lives, and is likely to be the greatest ideological battle of the post–cold-war era.

Where, then, does that leave us? The United States, an overwhelmingly non-Muslim country, obviously cannot fix the problems of the Muslim world. It can neither solve the trauma of modern Islam nor do a great deal even to reduce the anti-Americanism that is rife among Muslims. As the internal battle unfolds, non-Muslims will mostly find themselves in the role of outsiders.

But outsiders, and the United States in particular, can critically help in precipitating the battle and in influencing its outcome. They can do so both by weakening the militant side and by helping the moderate one. The process has in fact already begun in the so-called war on terrorism, and in miniature the results have been dramatically on display in Afghanistan. So long as Washington stayed aloof, the Taliban held sway in that country and the Northern Alliance appeared to be, and was, a hapless force. Once the U.S. military became involved, the Taliban crumbled and the Northern Alliance swept through the country in a few weeks. On the larger front the task is the same: weaken Islamists where they are in power, deter their expansion, and encourage and support moderate elements.

Weakening militant Islam will require an imaginative and assertive policy, one tailored to the needs of each country. Already the impress of American power has been felt in a number of places, from Afghanistan, where it toppled a government, to the Philippines, where $93 million in military and security aid, plus a contingent of advisers, is helping the government defeat a militant Islamic insurgency. In Pakistan, the FBI is training immigration officers to detect suspected terrorists infiltrating from Afghanistan. The anarchic areas of Somalia may be next on the list. . . .

When it comes to Islam, the U.S. role is less to offer its

own views than to help those Muslims with compatible views, especially on such issues as relations with non-Muslims, modernization, and the rights of women and minorities. This means helping moderates get their ideas out on U.S.-funded radio stations like the newly-created Radio Free Afghanistan and, as Paula Dobriansky, the Undersecretary of State for global affairs, has suggested, making sure that tolerant Islamic figures—scholars, imams, and others—are included in U.S.-funded academic- and cultural-exchange programs.

Anti-Islamists today are weak, divided, intimidated, and generally ineffectual. Indeed, the prospects for Muslim revitalization have rarely looked dimmer than at this moment of radicalism, jihad, extremist rhetoric, conspiratorial thinking, and the cult of death. But moderates do exist, and they have much to offer the United States in its own battle against militant Islam, not least their intimate knowledge of the phenomenon and of its potential weaknesses. In addition, the legitimacy they bring to any campaign against militant Islam, simply by rendering the charge of "Islamophobia" unsustainable, is invaluable.

In Afghanistan, the United States first crushed the Taliban regime, then turned the country over to the more moderate Northern Alliance; it is up to the Alliance to make something of the opportunity the U.S. created. The same holds with Islam writ large. Washington can go only so far. Whether its military victories turn into political ones depends ultimately on Muslims. The fight against militant Islam will be won if America has the will and persistence to see it through, and the wit to understand that its message must be carried in the end by other hands than its own.

The United States Should Maintain a Long-Term Military Presence in Central Asia

Charles Fairbanks

Following the September 11 attacks, the United States began using air bases in the nations of Central Asia, including Uzbekistan and Kyrgyzstan, to stage their war against the Taliban in Afghanistan. In the following article, Charles Fairbanks argues that despite the risks of stationing U.S. military personnel in these nations, the United States should maintain a military presence in Central Asia for several years. He contends that a U.S. presence in these states will prevent terrorist groups from thriving in the region and will help stabilize Afghanistan. Fairbanks is a professor at the Johns Hopkins School of Advanced International Studies.

The United States has refrained from giving explicit security guarantees in exchange for access to Central Asian bases and staging areas, but the mere presence of U.S. forces under present circumstances suggests commitment. Such a suggestion abides, too, in the U.S.-Uzbekistan joint declaration of March 12, 2002, on a "Strategic Partnership and Cooperation Framework." That declaration reads, in part, that the United States "affirms that it would regard with grave concern any external threat to the security and territorial integrity of the Republic of Uzbekistan." Commitment is also implied in the amplified military-to-military relationships that normally and naturally accompany the provision of U.S. military aid.

Will this commitment wax or wane? Should it wax or wane? These are difficult questions, and the Bush Adminis-

Charles Fairbanks, "Being There," *National Interest*, Summer 2002, pp. 39–53. Copyright © 2002 by The National Interest. Reproduced by permission.

tration is now called upon to answer them. The key issue is the U.S. military presence; this is what most concerns the major powers that border Central Asia—Russia, China and Iran—and what symbolizes most vividly the expansion of U.S. global power to others worldwide. It is also the most important factor in creating U.S. political debts to local host governments.

Good arguments can be made both for and against a long-term U.S. military presence. On balance, however, the more prudent course would be to anticipate, and not to dread, several years' military basing in Central Asia. Military training relationships will make sense for decades. But we should acknowledge the potential dangers in such a course, the better to mitigate them to the extent possible. There are four such dangers.

The Dangers of a U.S. Presence in Central Asia

First, none of the five Central Asian governments is a democracy, and most are plunged in an economic crisis comparable to the Great Depression. Polls suggest that these weaknesses threaten the legitimacy of several governments. Clearly, these governments will wish to use the U.S. need for access to their territory to slacken pressure on them with regard to political and economic reform. Worse, aid money provided to autocratic governments may exacerbate corruption, making better governance more difficult instead of less. They will also try to leverage their relationship with the United States in their regional rivalries with each other. And, of course, the United States risks being associated with unpopular regimes in the eyes of the peoples of these countries, and suffering when those regimes eventually fall.

Second, there are possible military costs as well as benefits from a protracted Central Asian deployment. A prolonged presence in Central Asia could expose U.S. forces to Islamist guerrilla attack. Moreover, the Pentagon is preoccupied by the strain on military effectiveness created by the increased dispersal of its forces. With the substantial contraction of the Services since the end of the Cold War, and a general unwillingness to provide a defense budget that is adequate for both existing forces and force modernization, this is a serious concern.

Third is the potential impact of a protracted Central Asian deployment on U.S. relationships with major powers, notably Russia, China and Iran. The sudden arrival of the American military next door—in Afghanistan, Uzbekistan and Kyrgyzstan—along with the upsurge of Palestinian terrorism and Israeli reaction, appears to have outweighed Iranian interest in detente with the United States. From an opportunity to escape isolation, America has become, in Iranian clerical eyes, the very country tightening an iron ring around Iran. Central Asian regimes will try to use the American presence to ward off burdensome pressures from Russia and China; we will therefore become enmeshed in a test of wills guaranteed to irritate one side or the other— maybe both. In the Russian case, a long-term American deployment would abrade the Russian sense of historical entitlement in Central Asia. The Russians—government elite and the public alike—may also claim a swindle: Just as the United States, they believe, reneged on a solemn promise not to expand NATO in the context of the agreement on German re-unification, so the Americans have taken advantage of Russian support for a temporary U.S. use of Central Asian facilities in the context of the war on terrorism to put Russia at a permanent geostrategic disadvantage. China worries that a protracted U.S. presence in Central Asia is part of an effort at encirclement and containment. There is a range of issues on which the United States seeks cooperation with Russia, China and Iran, and their displeasure over the U.S. presence in Central Asia could make securing that cooperation more difficult and expensive.

Finally, perhaps the most serious bundle of problems with staying involves not Russians or Chinese but ourselves. We are woefully ignorant about the area and, worse, our ignorance tends to be filled by wishful thinking. To substitute our daydreams, like the Middle East "peace process", for real knowledge of people and their cultures is one of the more unfortunate American traits.

These four dangers in staying constitute real potential

weaknesses. But leaving is even more dangerous. Like it or not, the United States finds itself in a situation where it must extend itself into the world in various places and ways if it is to meet the security challenges posed by apocalyptic terrorism joined to the proliferation of weapons of mass destruction. If the United States is going to succeed in the effort the President has put before the country, we must acknowledge that risks must be taken and prices must be paid. Whether done more in sorrow than in joy it does not matter; we must re-examine the scope not only of our foreign policy and defense policy, but of our entire contact with the world.

The United States Must Stabilize Central Asia

The United States must stay in Central Asia, militarily and otherwise, for essentially three interconnected reasons. First, the nature and scope of international terrorism is broader than many appreciate. A critical part of the problem is that weak states abet terrorism, and Central Asia is home to several weak states.

Second, the United States stands to benefit enormously in the long run from the increased stability and the success of moderate Muslim societies and states. Central Asian Islam is for reasons of history and happenstance more moderate than most other types, and it is worth our effort to sustain that moderation.

Third, we need to stay in Central Asia in order to stabilize Afghanistan. The idea that it will be enough to smash the Taliban and give humanitarian aid to render the country essentially harmless to American security is wrong. It will be hard to stabilize that country, and it will not be accomplished anytime soon. Moreover, because of Afghanistan's geopolitical situation—bordering Iran, Pakistan, Uzbekistan, Turkmenistan, Tajikistan and China—it is a far more important country than even most American foreign policy experts tend to appreciate.

Islamist Terrorism and Weak States

The Bush Administration has waged war with inflexible resolution and inventiveness, but it has not cast much light on the real problem we face with international terrorism. Because certain bureaucracies were habituated to narrowly define the problem as singularly that of Al-Qaeda, the preconditions of Al-Qaeda's success have remained obscure. In fact, the problem of Islamist terrorism is fourfold.

The existence of small fanatical groups of full-time terrorists is only the first part of it. A second precondition is a climate of opinion in the Muslim world that tolerates preaching and recruitment for such groups. Third, such groups need sponsors, which Saudis, aided by a double-gaming Saudi state, were for Al-Qaeda and Pakistan was for the Taliban. To operate effectively, terrorists also need seams between state administrations where they can operate without their sponsors being identified or taking responsibility. So, fourth and finally, the terrorists require places to host them, such as Taliban Afghanistan, and before Afghanistan Sudan, and still to this day Syria and its Lebanese satrapy. In other words, terrorism needs failed or weak states to thrive.

This becomes clear if we review the prewar situation in Afghanistan. The Taliban sympathized with Al-Qaeda's interpretation of Islam, though only in general terms. In the course of the war, however, it became clear that the Taliban also needed Al-Qaeda: to supply highly motivated troops in the absence of a real Taliban army; to give money in the absence of a state apparatus that could raise or manage money; and to supply ignorant village mullahs with ideological guidance, as Al-Qaeda's role in the destruction of the Bamiyan Buddhas suggests. Put differently, the Taliban needed Al-Qaeda because they lacked a state in the modern sense, even though such an organization would be outlawed under normal circumstances. Al-Qaeda needed a place where state structures had been destroyed by civil conflict and left unredressed by international assistance.

Weak states in general pose serious problems for American foreign policy, but our realpolitik orientation on powerful states often obscures this fact. If we list the major headaches of U.S. foreign policy since the end of the Cold War, we find that more have come from weak states such as Bosnia and Haiti than from powerful states like China. September 11 has shown the need for a major re-focusing of U.S. foreign policy to deal with such neglected cases because weak states that happen also to be Muslim states are prime locales for terrorist refuges. It is no accident that Somalia, Puntland (an unrecognized government within the former Somalia) and Yemen became the foci of American concern after the initial victories in Afghanistan. Few have remarked, however, on how much these places resemble each other.

Of course, there are many patches of this planet that lack normal, functioning states in the modern sense. Aside from Somalia and Yemen, we may name the Democratic Republic of the Congo, Liberia, Sierra Leone, Georgia, Bosnia, Colombia, Iraq and others. It is no surprise that within these states are areas not recognized as states that fulfill the conditions for terrorism noted above—places such as the Republika Srpska and Herzeg-Bosna within Bosnia; Abkhazia, South Ossetia and Achara within Georgia; Chechnya within the Russian Federation; the Kurdish quasi-governments in northern Iraq; and FARC- (and paramilitary) controlled areas of Colombia.

Weak states that provide administration-free zones are open not only to fanatics but to criminals and drug lords, as well. Afghanistan is the source of the bulk of the world's heroin, and most of it passes through Central Asia. Moreover, the decay of government authority in Central Asia is already a reality in some states and a possibility in all of them, particularly in remote mountainous areas that have always been recalcitrant to central control. The potential for such Muslim areas to provide religious fanatics and havens and to tempt state sponsors—three of the elements of Islamist terrorism—is very high.

This is already an urgent problem. Tajikistan and Kyrgyzstan are on the verge of failed-state status. When the Islamic Movement of Uzbekistan (IMU), a terrorist organization made up of many different nationalities, invaded Kyrgyzstan a few years ago with a few hundred fighters, the Kyrgyz government was unable to dislodge them. They finally left after an enormous bribe. This disaster was the result of President Askar Akaev's failure to build a normal army, the historical precondition of a modern state. Shoring up the feeble statehood of several Central Asian states is an important anti-terrorist task for the United States, and nothing we can do to this end is as important as training combat-capable armed forces. We began doing this quietly after the IMU incursion, but the pace and scope of this aid has greatly increased since September 11. We need to see this process through to success. This will take time, and it will be facilitated immensely by a local U.S. military presence.

Finally on this point, weak states in the former Soviet Union are a particular problem for the United States. This is because we have treated the map that came into being at the end of 1991 as a permanent international settlement, like the negotiated settlements of 1815 and 1919. We regard those borders as permanent, but several states there, including Tajikistan, do not control all their nominal territory. That heightens the stakes of our general diplomatic posture of support for the consolidation of independent statehood in Central Asia along invariant territorial lines. Russian attempts to "reintegrate" the former Soviet Union, such as they are, run counter to our diplomatic design. We can affect Russian behavior, however, not only by negotiating with them but by changing the facts with which they work. Stronger states in Central Asia will diminish Russia's interest in a revisionist foreign policy. Thus, a policy aimed primarily at preventing and deterring terrorism can work at the same time as a bulwark against lingering imperial tendencies in Russian foreign policy.

The Value of Moderate Muslim Countries

Because the general atmosphere of Muslim countries provides an atmosphere conducive to anti-American terrorism, the United States has a great stake in the success of Muslim states with a moderate orientation. Muslims regard Islam as an umma-a single community—and the points of view that exist within it are important for the direction that the community as a whole will take. This is the reason that Israel has expended such effort to cultivate the Central Asian states. A similar effort should serve us as well.

We start with a major advantage. Traditional Islam in Central Asia never took the Wahhabi form that most often supplies the doctrinal element in contemporary Islamist terrorism. Attachment to formal as opposed to folk or Sufi Islam was never strong among the nomads, the ancestors of the Kazakhs, Kyrgyz and Turkmen, and the Soviet period made the ruling elites of every republic very secular in orientation. Central Asian elites understand and even exaggerate the danger of some forms of Islam to their new states. People are currently rediscovering Islam, some as cultural identity, some in traditional form, and a few as political extremists. But having suffered intra-ethnic violence and seen civil war in Tajikistan, nearly everyone is wary of anything that might spark fighting on a sectarian basis. Thus the Central Asian states, if they can become strong states, can provide significant support for our conception of international order: culturally diverse but tolerant and peaceful.

Closely related to such a conception is the more general American desire to help people, which is not only noble but self-interested. America and its friends account for some 78 percent of "gross world product." September 11 was a sign that the accumulation of American power has reached a point where almost all enemies will respond to us asymmetrically: that is, outside the traditional arena of world politics. America, like Rome at the end of the Second Punic War, seems to be turning into the kernel of a world empire. The only thing that can make a world empire acceptable, however, is some kind of beneficence. Policies such as ending the slave trade made Britain's position in the first half of the 19th century more legitimate. Beneficence—for us, assistance to those who want to be free, action for human rights and democracy, and tolerance—sometimes crosses other foreign policy aims, and it always runs the risk of hypocrisy. But it is still important. A policy to work intensively with the existing Central Asian regimes may be justified by national interest, but it requires as well an active concern for the long-term encouragement of positive trends in these societies.

Unless we act more seriously than we have in the recent past, however, our effort at improvement will indeed seem hypocritical. The United States, the most influential democratic country, routinely protests the lack of free elections in places like Turkmenistan, where the question of elections has no practical relevance. But we do nothing effective in cases where the question is current, where there is international leverage for positive change, and where we would pay only a small price for greater activism. Kyrgyzstan, for example, began as the most democratic country in Central Asia, but has strayed from the path. Enormous foreign debt, which cannot be repaid, dependence on foreign aid and international investment, and the threat of extreme Islamist groups give the democratic community enormous leverage in Bishkek. Major geopolitical interests are scarcely at issue. Nonetheless, democratic countries have passively observed the dimming of Kyrgyzstan's democratic prospects. When President Akaev's major rival, former Bishkek mayor Felix Kulov, was prevented by various shenanigans from actively contesting the 2000 presidential election, the only American responses were private ambassadorial remonstrances, a brief scolding from visiting Secretary of State Madeleine Albright, and a testy phrase or two in a State Department press briefing. There were no concrete consequences.

U.S. human rights policy needs to differentiate its strategies toward various countries, seeking objectives that are obtainable. Free elections are conceivable in Kyrgyzstan, and they might change the nature of the system. Free elections are impossible for years under the present Uzbek or Turkmen regimes, so we should not demand them. The registration of a human rights NGO [nongovernmental organization], on the other hand, was achieved in Uzbekistan in the circumstances of the new U.S.-Uzbek relationship after September 11. Sometimes governments will accept some risks in domestic relations if their external security seems to be better guaranteed, and this is the effect of our arrival on all the Central Asian states. We should leverage our presence to achieve feasible change and thereby strive to reduce over time the problem of working with Central Asia's authoritarian regimes.

Of course, interference in the ways of Central Asian rulers may sour their zeal for military cooperation. We can reduce our risk in this respect by maintaining several military relationships in the region. That will enable us to shift from one base to another if need be, remaining relatively detached from tense Central Asian rivalries. Countering all the inconveniences of their relationships with America, too, will be an eagerness to have us as a counterweight to post-colonial Russia.

There is always a danger in overstaying a welcome, but in Central Asia today there is a danger of understaying a welcome, too. Just as it proved unwise to abandon Afghanistan after the withdrawal of the Red Army in 1989, so it would be a mistake to give up too soon trying to help Central Asian states become forces for moderation and stability in the Muslim world.

Stabilizing Afghanistan

Most important of all, it will prove extremely difficult, if not impossible, to stabilize Afghanistan without a military presence in the former Soviet republics to the north. Weak or failed states foster terrorism, especially if they are Muslim; if Afghanistan is prey to the lawlessness, misery and statelessness that now exist, then the Taliban, or another group like it, will rise again in a few years, attract groups such as Al-Qaeda and we will face September 11—or worse—all over again.

Our task in Afghanistan, which the Bush Administration understands well, is to restore the economy by a route other than renewed opium production, to build an Afghan state that can control Taliban remnants, and to educate Pashtun youth to a more centrist version of Islam. There has been scant recognition so far, however, on just how difficult this task will be.

To do any of this, America needs stability in Afghanistan, and no stability is possible without some approximate balance between the competing ethnic factions within the country and their foreign patrons. The interim government is "multiethnic", but bureaucratic titles mean little in a country that has been hacked apart by civil war for thirty years. In such a situation the "power ministries", to use the expressive post-Soviet jargon, are decisive. Mohammed Fahim and Yonus Qanuni, the Ministers of Defense and Interior, are the masters, along with their close ally, Foreign Minister Abdullah. The way they use their mastery is eloquently expressed by their choice of generals for the new "national" army: 36 of the initial 38 generals were Tajiks, most of them, like Fahim, Qanuni and Abdullah, of Panjshiri background.

Postwar Afghanistan is so far an endeavor to dominate fourteen or more discordant ethnic and religious groups not by the Northern Alliance, nor by Tajiks, nor even by Sunni Tajiks, but by Panjshiri Sunni Tajiks—the inhabitants of just one valley in a very big country. Such a project will inevitably invite the hostility of most other ethnic groups and factions. Moreover, because every Afghan group has a foreign patron, this audacious attempt throws the equilibrium among foreign states out of balance. During the years of Taliban rule, the Northern Alliance depended predominantly on Russia and Iran. Iran now plays a more independent game in western Afghanistan, but the Panjshiris still look to Russia.

The Russian government has taken advantage of U.S. military victories in Afghanistan to pursue objectives there that are directly opposed to America's own policy and interests. With the Panjshiri Tajiks as their utensils, Moscow essays again the establishment of preponderant Russian influence over Afghan affairs. The Russian project in Afghanistan is staggering in its boldness. When there was a Soviet Union, something similar was tried with the instrument of Afghan communism, and then with an army that had overawed all of Eurasia. Now, shrunken Russia—with an economy contracted to less than South Korean dimensions, a weakened state and a demoralized army—tries again. It is hardly child's play. The mischief being done by Russia in Afghanistan should be considered when we weigh the utility—and the future—of our Central Asian military presence.

The War on Terrorism Should Extend to Iraq

Gary Schmitt

In the following selection, Gary Schmitt, executive director of the Project for the New American Century, argues
that the Iraqi regime of Saddam Hussein poses a severe
terrorist threat and should therefore be overturned. He
insists that the terrorists behind the September 11, 2001,
attacks on America had ties to high-level Iraqi officials. In
addition, Iraq is pursuing the development of weapons of
mass destruction—including nuclear, chemical, and biological weapons—with an intent to use them against the
United States. For these reasons, according to Schmitt,
the war on terrorism must include the demise of Hussein's
rule as one of its goals.

Subsequent to the writing of the following article, U.S.
president George W. Bush announced that he supported
regime change in Iraq—by force if necessary. In December 2002 the United Nations, under U.S. pressure, re-
sumed weapons inspections in Iraq, which had been suspended in 1998.

Shortly before getting on a plane to fly to New Jersey from
Europe in June 2000, Mohamed Atta, the lead hijacker of
the first jet airliner to slam into the World Trade Center
and, apparently, the lead conspirator in the attacks of September 11, 2001, met with a senior Iraqi intelligence official.
This was no chance encounter. Rather than take a flight
from Germany, where he had been living, Atta traveled to
Prague, almost certainly for the purpose of meeting there
with Iraqi intelligence operative Ahmed Samir Ahani.

To understand the significance of this meeting, put yourself in the position of a terrorist. You work within a small cell of operatives; you are continually concerned about security; and you are about to launch a mission designed to bring unprecedented death and destruction to the world's most powerful country. The last thing you would do would be to meet with a foreign official—especially one from a country whose "diplomats" are presumably under close surveillance—unless the meeting were critical to your mission. In light of the otherwise sound "trade-craft" demonstrated by Atta and his confederates in the run-up to September 11, Atta would never have met with an Iraqi intelligence officer unless the Iraqi had been in some way in on the operation.

A Smoking Gun

U.S. intelligence officials have responded to reports of this meeting (and others between Atta and Iraqi intelligence operatives) by denying that they provide a smoking gun tying Iraq to the attacks of September 11. That might be true by the standards of a court of law, but the United States is now engaged not in legal wrangling but in a deadly game of espionage and terrorism. In the world where we now operate, the Prague meeting is about as clear and convincing as evidence gets—especially since our intelligence service apparently has no agents in place of its own to tell us what was in fact going on.

This much, however, is beyond dispute: Regardless of the differences between their visions for the Middle East, Saddam Hussein and Osama bin Laden share an overriding objective—to expel the United States from the Middle East. Alliances have been built on less.

And there is evidence of an alliance. For example, there are numerous reports that Saddam's henchmen were reaching out to bin Laden as early as the early 1990s, when he was still operating out of Sudan and Iraq was using Khartoum as a base for its own intelligence operations after the Gulf War. We also know that high-ranking Iraqi intelligence officials have made their way to Afghanistan in recent years to meet with bin Laden and the leadership of al Qaeda. There are

Iraqi defectors who claim to have seen radical Muslims at a special terrorist training site in Iraq where trainees learn, among other things, to hijack airplanes. None of this should be a surprise. Iraq can offer bin Laden money and technical expertise, and in exchange al Qaeda can provide the manpower to strike at the United States without exposing Baghdad's hand.

Iraq and Unconventional Weapons

Then there is the matter of the refined anthrax that was used against American media in Florida and against Congress in the letter sent to Senator Tom Daschle's office. (Both attacks, by the way, came from places visited by Mohamed Atta, New Jersey and Florida.) As Ambassador Richard Butler, former head of the United Nations weapons-inspection effort for Iraq after the Gulf War, has said, "I don't believe that the terrorist groups—al Qaeda and Osama bin Laden—could themselves make anthrax" of this quality. Iraq could. Since the defection of Hussein Kamal, Saddam Hussein's son-in-law, in 1995, we have known that Iraq retains a large biological weapons program. We know it has stockpiled mass quantities of anthrax and has worked hard to make it as potent a weapon of terror as possible.

That Iraq would have a hand in the September 11 attacks or the subsequent anthrax onslaught or both should come as no surprise. [Experts later determined that the anthrax attacks were most likely the work of a domestic terrorist.] Since 1991, Saddam has been at war with the United States, and we with him. The Iraqi dictator has made it known time and again that the "mother of all battles" continues. And, like all tyrants of his maniacal stripe, he seeks not simply to hold onto power but to claim a place in history. As a result, Saddam will never relent until he has had his revenge and driven the United States from the Persian Gulf.

Every so often, we are reminded that the war continues, when Iraq attempts to shoot down an American or British fighter flying over the no-fly zones in northern and southern Iraq and we in turn bomb an Iraqi air-defense site. If this were all the war amounted to, one could argue that containing Saddam within Iraq sufficed for our strategic purposes. But it's not. In 1993, Saddam ordered his intelligence services to assassinate former President George Bush on his trip to Kuwait. Moreover, there are good reasons to believe that Iraq had a hand in the first World Trade Center bombing back in 1993. The mastermind behind the plot was linked to Iraq (via a passport and other details), and a second key figure in the bombing fled soon afterwards to Iraq. Although the Clinton administration ignored the links to Iraq and refused to follow them up, Jim Fox, the FBI's head agent in New York at the time, was convinced of Iraq's involvement. And, finally, we know that Saddam's Iraq continues to pursue development of weapons of mass destruction—nuclear, chemical, and biological—believing that these are the ultimate keys to overcoming America's military dominance in the region.

In short, Iraq is both equipped with dangerous weapons and out to get the United States. If we have learned one lesson from bin Laden, it is that when someone says he is at war with you, and he has the tools to cause you significant harm, it's no longer enough to say you are watching him carefully. The potential costs of leaving Saddam and his regime in place are simply too high.

Mere Containment Is Not Wise

This conclusion of course is not shared on all sides. Some still insist that we can contain Iraq, just as we contained the Soviet Union for more than four decades. After all, the Soviet Union posed a far greater threat than Iraq today. But this assumes that containment was our preferred strategic policy during the Cold War. It wasn't. Containment was born of necessity—initially, a lack of conventional forces capable of defeating the Red Army in the drawdown following World War II, and subsequently, the threat of the Soviet Union's own nuclear weapons. If we don't have to adopt a policy of containment, we shouldn't.

Moreover, if all we do is contain Saddam's Iraq, it is a virtual certainty that Baghdad will soon have nuclear weapons. (German intelligence believes that day may come within three years.) The question any serious statesman must ask himself is how Saddam, once nuclear-armed, is likely to behave. Will he at that point think we have the stomach to play the game of nuclear deterrence on behalf of our allies in the region, if deterring him could cost us our own massive casualties? It's a risk no one should want to take.

Right now of course the major stumbling block to taking on Iraq in this war, we are told, is the absence of support from our coalition partners for such a course. But that's because they have their doubts, with some justification, that we would be serious about finishing off Saddam. The fact is, the old Persian Gulf coalition began to fall apart around the time the Clinton administration failed to defend the CIA-supported Iraqi opposition from an attack by Saddam's forces in 1996. From that day forward, it was clear that the United States was not really serious, and every state was out for itself. If Washington shows that it intends to get rid of Saddam, the allies who matter will be with us.

There is no question that Iraq has been involved in terrorism in the past; and there is more evidence that it has engaged in terrorism against the United States than many in Washington are willing to admit. But the far more important justification for extending the war on terrorism to toppling Saddam's regime is the terrorist threat he will pose in the near future when his efforts to acquire still deadlier weapons come to fruition. The present war provides President George W. Bush with the opportunity to prevent this from happening. But it is an opportunity that will not last for long. If two or three years from now Saddam is still in power, the war on terrorism will have failed.

Appendix of Documents

Document 1: President Bush Addresses the Nation After the September 11 Attacks

On the evening of September 11, 2001, the president stressed the evil nature of the attacks and said that Americans would respond with "quiet, unyielding anger."

Good evening. Today, our fellow citizens, our way of life, our very freedom came under attack in a series of deliberate and deadly terrorist acts. The victims were in airplanes, or in their offices; secretaries, businessmen and women, military and federal workers; moms and dads, friends and neighbors. Thousands of lives were suddenly ended by evil, despicable acts of terror.

The pictures of airplanes flying into buildings, fires burning, huge structures collapsing, have filled us with disbelief, terrible sadness, and a quiet, unyielding anger. These acts of mass murder were intended to frighten our nation into chaos and retreat. But they have failed; our country is strong.

A great people has been moved to defend a great nation. Terrorist attacks can shake the foundations of our biggest buildings, but they cannot touch the foundation of America. These acts shattered steel, but they cannot dent the steel of American resolve.

America was targeted for attack because we're the brightest beacon for freedom and opportunity in the world. And no one will keep that light from shining.

Today, our nation saw evil, the very worst of human nature. And we responded with the best of America—with the daring of our rescue workers, with the caring for strangers and neighbors who came to give blood and help in any way they could.

Immediately following the first attack, I implemented our government's emergency response plans. Our military is powerful, and it's prepared. Our emergency teams are working in New York City and Washington, D.C., to help with local rescue efforts.

Our first priority is to get help to those who have been injured, and to take every precaution to protect our citizens at home and around the world from further attacks.

The functions of our government continue without interruption. Federal agencies in Washington which had to be evacuated today are reopening for essential personnel tonight, and will be open for business tomorrow. Our financial institutions remain strong, and the American economy will be open for business, as well.

The search is underway for those who are behind these evil acts. I've directed the full resources of our intelligence and law enforcement communities to find those responsible and to bring them to justice. We will make no distinction between the terrorists who committed these acts and those who harbor them.

I appreciate so very much the members of Congress who have joined me in strongly condemning these attacks. And on behalf of the American people, I thank the many world leaders who have called to offer their condolences and assistance.

America and our friends and allies join with all those who want peace and security in the world, and we stand together to win the war against terrorism. Tonight, I ask for your prayers for all those who grieve, for the children whose worlds have been shattered, for all whose sense of safety and security has been threatened. And I pray they will be comforted by a power greater than any of us, spoken through the ages in Psalm 23: "Even though I walk through the valley of the shadow of death, I fear no evil, for You are with me."

This is a day when all Americans from every walk of life unite in our resolve for justice and peace. America has stood down enemies before, and we will do so this time. None of us will ever forget this day. Yet, we go forward to defend freedom and all that is good and just in our world.

Thank you. Good night, and God bless America.

George W. Bush, "Address to the Nation," September 11, 2001, www.whitehouse.gov.

Document 2: The British Government Blames al-Qaeda

The following excerpt from a British government report traces the link between al-Qaeda and the September 11 attacks.

Al Qaida is a terrorist organisation with ties to a global network, which has been in existence for over 10 years. It was founded, and has been led at all times, by Usama Bin Laden.

Usama Bin Laden and Al Qaida have been engaged in a jihad against the United States, and its allies. One of their stated aims is the murder of US citizens, and attacks on America's allies.

Usama Bin Laden and Al Qaida have been based in Afghanistan since 1996, but have a network of operations throughout the world. The network includes training camps, warehouses, communication facilities and commercial operations able to raise significant sums of money to support its activity. That activity includes substantial exploitation of the illegal drugs trade from Afghanistan.

Usama Bin Laden's Al Qaida and the Taleban régime have a close and mutually dependent alliance. Usama Bin Laden and Al Qaida provide the Taleban régime with material, financial and military support. They jointly exploit the drugs trade. The Taleban régime allows Bin Laden to operate his terrorist training camps and activities from Afghanistan, protects him from attacks from outside, and protects the drugs stockpiles. Usama Bin Laden could not operate his terrorist activities without the alliance and support of the Taleban régime. The Taleban's strength would be seriously weakened without Usama Bin Laden's military and financial support.

Usama Bin Laden and Al Qaida have the capability to execute major terrorist attacks.

Usama Bin Laden has claimed credit for the attack on US soldiers in Somalia in October 1993, which killed 18; for the attack on the US Embassies in Kenya and Tanzania in August 1998 which killed 224 and injured nearly 5000; and was linked to the attack on the USS Cole on 12 October 2000, in which 17 crew members were killed and 40 others injured.

They have sought to acquire nuclear and chemical materials for use as terrorist weapons.

In relation to the terrorist attacks on 11 September:

After 11 September we learned that, not long before, Bin Laden had indicated he was about to launch a major attack on America. The detailed planning for the terrorist attacks of 11 September was carried out by one of UBL's close associates. Of the 19 hijackers involved in 11 September 2001, it has been established that the majority had links with Al Qaida. A senior Bin Laden associate claimed to have trained some of the hijackers in Afghanistan. The attacks on 11 September 2001 were similar in both their ambition and intended impact to previous attacks undertaken by Usama Bin Laden and Al Qaida, and also had features in common. In particular:

• Suicide attackers
• Co-ordinated attacks on the same day
• The aim to cause maximum American casualties
• Total disregard for other casualties, including Muslim
• Meticulous long-term planning
• Absence of warning.

Al Qaida retains the capability and the will to make further at-

tacks on the US and its allies, including the United Kingdom.
Al Qaida gives no warning of terrorist attack.

Government of the United Kingdom of Great Britain and Northern Ireland, "Responsibility for the Terrorist Atrocities in the United States, 11 September 2001—An Updated Account," November 14, 2001, www.pm.gov.uk.

Document 3: Osama bin Laden Condemns the United States

In an interview with reporter Peter L. Bergen, Osama bin Laden denounces what he sees as America's imperialism in the Arab and Muslim countries. His stated goal is to drive the U.S. presence from Muslim countries.

When you go looking for Osama bin Laden, you don't find him: he finds you. It was March 1997 when the phone rang.

"Osama has agreed to meet with you in Afghanistan," said the voice at the other end of the line.

Bin Laden and his advisers had concluded that CNN, my then employer, was the best forum to broadcast his first television interview to the English-speaking world. . . .

Without raising his voice, bin Laden began to rail in Arabic against the injustices visited upon Muslims by the United States and his native Saudi Arabia: "Our main problem is the U.S. government. . . . By being loyal to the U.S. regime, the Saudi regime has committed an act against Islam," he said. Bin Laden made no secret of the fact that he was interested in fomenting a revolution in Saudi Arabia, and that his new regime would role in accordance with the seventh-century precepts of the Prophet Muhammad. "We are confident . . . that Muslims will be victorious in the Arabian peninsula and that God's religion, praise and glory be to Him, will prevail in this peninsula. It is a great . . . hope that the revelation unto Muhammad will be used for ruling."

Bin Laden coughed softly throughout the interview and nursed a cup of tea. No doubt he was suffering from a cold brought on by the drafty Afghan mountains. He continued on in his soft-spoken but focused manner, an ambiguous, thin smile sometimes playing on his lips: "We declared jihad against the U.S. government because the U.S. government . . . has committed acts that are extremely unjust, hideous, and criminal whether directly or through its support of the Israeli occupation of [Palestine]. And we believe the U.S. is directly responsible for those who were killed in Palestine, Lebanon, and Iraq. This U.S. government abandoned humanitarian feelings by these hideous crimes. It transgressed all bounds and behaved in a way not witnessed before by any power or any imperialist power in the world. Due to its subordination to the Jews, the arrogance and haughtiness of the U.S. regime has reached to the extent that they occupied [Arabia]. For this and other acts of aggression and injustice, we have declared jihad against the U.S., because in our religion it is our duty to make jihad so that God's word is the one exalted to the heights and so that we drive the Americans away from all Muslim countries."

Peter L. Bergen, *Holy War Inc.: Inside the Secret World of Osama bin Laden.* New York: Free Press, 2001.

Document 4: Transcript of Osama bin Laden Videotape

In mid-November 2001 Osama bin Laden was seen in a videotape in which he claimed responsibility for the World Trade Center attacks, described the goals of the attacks, and expressed thanks that his plan had achieved its aim. Bin Laden was conversing with an unidentified "Shayk," who appears to be crippled from the waist down. The Shayk expressed his happiness at the results of the attacks.

Usama bin Laden (UBL): Those youth who conducted the operations did not accept any fiqh, [literal definition is first jurisprudence], in the popular terms, but they accepted the fiqh that the prophet Muhammad brought. Those young men (. . . *inaudible* . . .) said in deeds, in New York and Washington, speeches that overshadowed all other speeches made everywhere else in the world. The speeches are understood by both Arabs and non-Arabs—even by Chinese. It is above all the media said. Some of them said that in Holland, at one of the centers, the number of people who accepted Islam during the days that followed the operations were more than the people who accepted Islam in the last eleven years. I heard someone on Islamic radio who owns a school in America say: "We don't have time to keep up with the demands of those who are asking about Islamic books to learn about Islam." This event made people think (*about true Islam*) which benefited Islam greatly.

Shaykh: Hundreds of people used to doubt you and few only would follow you until this huge event happened. Now hundreds of people are coming out to join you. I remember a vision by Shaykh Salih Al-(Shuaybi). He said: "There will be a great hit and people will go out by hundreds to Afghanistan." I asked him (*Salih*): "To Afghanistan?" He replied, "Yes." According to him, the only ones who stay behind will be the mentally impotent and the liars (*hypocrites*). I remembered his saying that hundreds of people will go out to Afghanistan. He had this vision a year ago. This event discriminated between the different types of followers.

UBL: (. . . *Inaudible* . . .) we calculated in advance the number of casualties from the enemy, who would be killed based on the position of the tower. We calculated that the floors that would be hit would be three or four floors. I was the most optimistic of them all. (. . . *Inaudible* . . .) due to my experience in this field, I was thinking that the fire from the gas in the plane would melt the iron structure of the building and collapse the area where the plane hit and all the floors above it only. This is all that we had hoped for.

Shaykh: Allah be praised.

UBL: We were at (. . . *inaudible* . . .) when the event took place. We had notification since the previous Thursday that the event would take place that day. We had finished our work that day and had the radio on. It was 5:30 p.m. our time. I was sitting with Dr. Ahmad Abu-al-(Khair). Immediately, we heard the news that a plane had hit the World Trade Center. We turned the radio station to the news from Washington. The news continued and no mention of the attack until the end. At the end of the newscast, they reported that a plane just hit the World Trade Center.

Shaykh: Allah be praised.

UBL: After a little while, they announced that another plane had hit the World Trade Center. The brothers who heard the news were overjoyed by it.

Shaykh: I listened to the news and I was sitting. We didn't . . . we were not thinking about anything, and all of a sudden, Allah willing, we were talking about how come we didn't have anything, and all of a sudden the news came and everyone was overjoyed and everyone until the next day, in the morning, was talking about what was happening and we stayed until four o'clock, listening to the news every time a little bit different, everyone was very joyous and saying "Allah is great," "Allah is great," "We are thankful to Allah," "Praise Allah." And I was happy for the happiness of my brothers. That day the congratulations were coming on the phone non-stop. The mother was receiving phone calls continuously. Thank Allah. Allah is great, praise be to Allah.

(*Quoting the verse from the Quran*)

Shaykh: "Fight them, Allah will torture them, with your hands, he will torture them. He will deceive them and he will give you victory. Allah will forgive the believers, he is knowledgeable about everything."

Transcript prepared by George Michael and Dr. Kassem M. Wahba, released December 13, 2001, www.fas.org.

Document 5: Excerpt of a Letter from Nairobi Embassy Bomber Haroun Fazul to al-Qaeda Member Sharif El Hage

Haroun Fazul was a terrorist connected with bin Laden's al-Qaeda net-work who drove one of the explosive-filled trucks that attacked the U.S. embassy in Nairobi, Kenya. In the letter to Sharif El Hage, also con-nected with al-Qaeda, Fazul worries that American intelligence officials are close to uncovering the al-Qaeda network's operations in East Africa. The letter shows the global extent of al-Qaeda's network.

We can now state that the security position on the cell is at 100 percent danger. In this report, I will try to explain the reasons that make us feel that danger (way). I will also try to offer my recom-mendation to honored and wise high command which I know un-derstands everything and we hope it is seeking the best. There are many reasons that lead me to believe that the cell members in East Africa are in great danger, which leaves us no choice but to think and work hard to foil the enemy's plans who is working day and night to catch one of us or gather more information about any of us. (This report stems from the basic principle that) anyone who studies security matters seriously, will never handle anything care-lessly, regardless of how small or great it is, but will take all mat-ters seriously. As we have heard, seen and read that the "Hajj" (comments: reference to Usama bin Ladin) has declared the war on America and that was confirmed when we saw the interview that took place in Jalalabad in which the Shaykh stated the follow-ing points:

- declaring war upon America because it had appointed itself the policeman of the world.
- he had nothing to do with the two explosions in Saudi Arabia but he was glad they took place.
- my future plans will be heard in the radio stations.

(Above was made) in addition to other points which pleased us all, thank God. In fact America's goal in that interview was to slan-der the Shaykh in the American people's mind and open a new door (of attack). This is being done in order to pave the way to catch him without any domestic opposition from within the states. The interview showed the Shaykh's picture when he was in Af-ghanistan and on the war fronts and they were showing his picture when they were showing the dead bodies of the Jews in Palestine and the Americans in Somalia and Yemen. They have also shown the two explosions in Riyadh and connected them with his oppo-sition to the Saudi regime. After they described him as a rich businessman who owns millions of dollars, they accused him of being the major financier of the mujahedin "terrorists" in the world and that he has a huge multi-national army and had become America's primary target. They have also shown another film for the Shaykh on 10 August 1997 on the same network CNN. From all this talk, we understood that America is willing to move against the Shaykh or those who are associated with him. After that a lot of news were broadcasted about the Hajj and his followers in the radio and magazines. We then heard the news of his move with his family from Jalalabad to Qandahar; they even named the village where he lives with his family. We were surprised to read in one of the English newspapers which noted that America had sent a force of one thousand multi-national mercenaries to Pakistan to try and kidnap the Shaykh or Mr. 'Atif.

From all these developments we understood that there is a war on and the situation is dangerous and that anybody who is associated with the Hajj regardless of their position and their nationality are at risk. Also, the American forces carry kidnaping operations against anyone who threatens its national security and its citizens, and we have seen that when they kidnaped the Pakistani national from one of the border villages whereby while he was sleeping in one location he found himself the next morning in Washington.

My recommendation to my brothers in East Africa was to not be complacent regarding security matters and that they should know that now they have become America's primary target and that they should know that there is an American-Kenyan-Egyptian intelligence activity in Nairobi aiming to identify the names and residences of the members who are associated with the Shaykh since America knows well that the youth who lived in Somalia and were members of the Shaykh's cell are the ones who killed the Americans in Somalia. They know that since Kenya was the main gateway for those members, there must be a center in Kenya. Ahmed (Tawii) told me that he will talk to Taysir about the changes since we are really in danger. Our biggest problem is that our security situation here is very weak. I told him that the network will appreciate the changes (in security) since we are convinced one hundred percent that the Kenyan intelligence are aware about us and that indeed our security situation is extremely bad.

We read in the Kenyan newspaper the "standard" news of the arrest of five terrorists in Kenya. When DC Gharissa declared that news, I warned Ahmad (Madubi) that there is an intelligence operation in Kenya to identify the leaders and the foreigners who deal with them. We think there is American pressure on Kenya to search for the Arabs living in the area (country). Therefore, brother Sharif, please watch out and also let the brother engineers be careful and be advised that anyone of us could fall in the trap. If the engineers come down, it would be better if they did not contact me and God willing, I will try and visit them at their homes.

The last bit of news which almost made me explode (go crazy) and which I consider the primary cause of danger for the East Africa network (concerned) the following. (This was in conjunction with what) we read in one of the British newspapers "The Daily Telegraph" and which I have asked brother Tawfiq to buy from Nairobi after hearing on BBC on 2 August 1997. The gist of the news is this: "There is an individual from the bin Ladin finance department currently in the hands of the American Central Intelligence Agency "CIA" and also in the hands on the British intelligence service "MI6" and is in Saudi Arabia. He was delivered to them through the Saudi intelligence service during the middle of May. Along with him is another individual called "Jallud" who is an assistant to Usama and who may have cooperated with the Saudi government after he was arrested since May. The newspaper also mentioned that Sidi Tayib had advised the American intelligence service about the scope of distribution of money to various Arab communities who cooperate with al Shaykh in the United States especially in Brooklyn, New Jersey and Jersey City. This individual was also said to have given details about Usama's financial information in Afghanistan and Pakistan and how much was sent to London and to Detroit in America. The newspaper also linked this news with the Jerusalem bombing and the arrest of Lafi Khalil in New York and his colleague Abu Mayzi. The newspaper further discussed the current residence of Usama in Qandahar and the number of his wives and his description and age and mentioned that he is wanted in Britain because of the bombings in [France] during 1995 which it noted he had financed and which was conducted by the Algerians who were based there at the time. It also noted that he has a hand within the Saudi opposition movement in London known as the "Committee for the Defense of Legitimate Rights". Additionally, it also noted that he is wanted by the Egyptian government for his involvement in the attempted assassination against the Egyptian president in 1995 in Ethiopia as well as for his support of the blind Shaykh "'Imar 'Abd al-Rahman" who was targeting tourists in Egypt.

Haroun Fazul, "Letter to Sharif El Hage," n.d.

Document 6: The Emergence of Mass-Destruction Terrorism

In this excerpt from a report of the Library of Congress, Federal Research Division, Rex A. Hudson notes that scholars have described a change in the motivations of the most prominent terrorists. Before the end of the Cold War many terrorist groups were politically motivated. They planned strikes which brought attention but did not provoke worldwide condemnation. In the 1990s and beyond, religiously oriented terror groups became prominent. These groups, such as the Japanese cult Aum Shinrikyo or the Islamic group al-Qaeda, are more willing to cause civilian casualties because they see themselves in a religious battle with forces of evil that must be destroyed. The risk is even greater now that such groups possess weapons of mass destruction such as poison gas or biological warfare agents.

In the 1970s and 1980s, it was commonly assumed that terrorist use of weapons of mass destruction (WMD) would be counterproductive because such an act would be widely condemned. "Terrorists want a lot of people watching, not a lot of people dead," Brian Jenkins opined. Jenkins's premise was based on the assumption that terrorist behavior is normative, and that if they exceeded certain constraints and employed WMD they would completely alienate themselves from the public and possibly provoke swift and harsh retaliation. This assumption does seem to apply to certain secular terrorist groups. If a separatist organization such as the Provisional Irish Republic Army (PIRA) or the Basque Fatherland and Liberty (Euzkadi Ta Askatasuna—ETA), for example, were to use WMD, these groups would likely isolate their constituency and undermine sources of funding and political support. When the assumptions about terrorist groups not using WMD were made in the 1970s and 1980s, most of the terrorist groups making headlines were groups with political or nationalist-separatist agenda. Those groups, with some exceptions, such as the Japanese Red Army (JRA—Rengo Sekigun), had reason not to sabotage their ethnic bases of popular support or other domestic or foreign sympathizers of their cause by using WMD.

Trends in terrorism over the past three decades, however, have contradicted the conventional thinking that terrorists are averse to using WMD. It has become increasingly evident that the assumption does not apply to religious terrorist groups or millenarian cults. Indeed, since at least the early 1970s analysts, including (somewhat contradictorily) Jenkins, have predicted that the first groups to employ a weapon of mass destruction would be religious sects with a millenarian, messianic, or apocalyptic mindset.

When the conventional terrorist groups and individuals of the early 1970s are compared with terrorists of the early 1990s, a trend can be seen: the emergence of religious fundamentalist and new religious groups espousing the rhetoric of mass-destruction terrorism. In the 1990s, groups motivated by religious imperatives, such as Aum Shinrikyo, Hizballah, and al-Qaida, have grown and proliferated. These groups have a different attitude toward violence—one that is extranormative and seeks to maximize violence against the perceived enemy, essentially anyone who is not a fundamentalist Muslim or an Aum Shinrikyo member. Their outlook is one that divides the world simplistically into "them" and "us." With its sarin attack on the Tokyo subway system on March 20, 1995, the doomsday cult Aum Shinrikyo turned the prediction of terrorists using WMD into reality.

Beginning in the early 1990s, Aum Shinrikyo engaged in a systematic program to develop and use WMD. It used chemical or biological WMD in about a dozen largely unreported instances in the first half of the 1990s, although they proved to be no more effective—actually less effective—than conventional weapons because of the terrorists' ineptitude. Nevertheless, it was Aum Shinrikyo's sarin attack on the Tokyo subway on March 20, 1995, that showed the world how dangerous the mindset of a religious terrorist group could be. The attack provided convincing evidence that Aum Shinrikyo probably would not hesitate to use WMD in a U.S. city, if it had an opportunity to do so. These religiously motivated groups would have no reason to take "credit" for such an act of mass destruction, just as Aum Shinrikyo did not take credit for its attack on the Tokyo subway, and just as Osama bin Laden did not take credit for various acts of high-casualty terrorism against U.S. targets in the 1990s. Taking credit means asking for retaliation. Instead, it is enough for these groups to simply take private satisfaction in knowing that they have dealt a harsh blow to what they perceive to be the "Great Satan." Groups unlikely to be deterred by fear of public disapproval, such as Aum Shinrikyo, are the ones who seek chaos as an end in itself.

The contrast between key members of religious extremist groups such as Hizballah, al-Qaida, and Aum Shinrikyo and conventional terrorists reveals some general trends relating to the personal attributes of terrorists likely to use WMD in coming years. According to psychologist Jerrold M. Post, the most dangerous terrorist is likely to be the religious terrorist. Post has explained that, unlike the average political or social terrorist, who has a defined mission that is somewhat measurable in terms of media attention or government reaction, the religious terrorist can justify the most heinous acts "in the name of Allah," for example. One could add, "in the name of Aum Shinrikyo's Shoko Asahara."

Rex A. Hudson, *The Sociology and Psychology of Terrorism: Who Becomes a Terrorist and Why?* Washington, DC: Library of Congress Research Service, 1999.

Document 7: The Importance of Sharing Intelligence

Former Israeli prime minister Benjamin Netanyahu has offered a series of recommendations on how Western countries can fight terrorism. In this excerpt, the ex–Special Forces soldier says that greater sharing of intelligence between countries is necessary in the war against terror. By not sharing basic information, intelligence agencies in various countries, or even within one country, put lives at risk.

One of the central problems in the fight against international terrorism has traditionally been the hesitation of the security services of one nation to share information with foreign services. In this regard, countries have often viewed "their" terrorists as though they were the only terrorists worth fighting, while turning a blind eye to activities hostile to other governments. The trouble with this method is not only that it is of questionable morality; the fact is that it does not work. Terrorists hide behind the mutual suspicions between the Western security services, seeming to be attacking a particular nation when in fact they often view the entire West as a common society and a common enemy. Only through close coordination between law enforcement officials and the intelligence services of all free countries can a serious effort against international terrorism be successful.

It should be made clear that I am not speaking here of warnings of impending terrorist attacks. Those are now shared instantaneously by virtually all the intelligence agencies of the West. What is not shared is basic data about terrorist organizations, their membership and their operational structure. These "cards" are often withheld from the intelligence services of other countries (and sometimes even from a rival service in the *same* country) for two reasons: either to protect the source of the information or else, at least as often, out of a habitual organizational jealousy. But the absence of systematic sharing of intelligence is not a matter of petty one-upmanship. It greatly hinders each democracy as it struggles alone to get a full picture of terrorist activity directed against its citizens, with the inevitable result that lives are needlessly lost. If the democracies wish to successfully confront the new terrorism, there is no choice but for the scope of intelligence cooperation to be increased, and the scope of the jealousies reduced.

Benjamin Netanyahu, *Fighting Terrorism: How Democracies Can Defeat Domestic and International Terrorists*. New York: Farrar, Straus and Giroux, 1995.

Document 8: U.S. National Security Strategy Against Terrorism

In September 2002, the United States issued a new national security strategy authored by national security adviser Condoleeza Rice. Section III of the new strategy deals with the war on terrorism.

The United States of America is fighting a war against terrorists of global reach. The enemy is not a single political regime or person or religion or ideology. The enemy is terrorism—premeditated, politically motivated violence perpetrated against innocents.

In many regions, legitimate grievances prevent the emergence of a lasting peace. Such grievances deserve to be, and must be, addressed within a political process. But no cause justifies terror. The United States will make no concessions to terrorist demands and strike no deals with them. We make no distinction between terrorists and those who knowingly harbor or provide aid to them.

The struggle against global terrorism is different from any other war in our history. It will be fought on many fronts against a particularly elusive enemy over an extended period of time. Progress will come through the persistent accumulation of successes—some seen, some unseen.

Today our enemies have seen the results of what civilized nations can, and will, do against regimes that harbor, support, and use terrorism to achieve their political goals. Afghanistan has been liberated; coalition forces continue to hunt down the Taliban and al-Qaida. But it is not only this battlefield on which we will engage terrorists. Thousands of trained terrorists remain at large with cells in North America, South America, Europe, Africa, the Middle East, and across Asia.

Our priority will be first to disrupt and destroy terrorist organizations of global reach and attack their leadership; command, control, and communications; material support; and finances. This will have a disabling effect upon the terrorists' ability to plan and operate.

We will continue to encourage our regional partners to take up a coordinated effort that isolates the terrorists. Once the regional campaign localizes the threat to a particular state, we will help ensure the state has the military, law enforcement, political, and financial tools necessary to finish the task.

The United States will continue to work with our allies to disrupt the financing of terrorism. We will identify and block the sources of funding for terrorism, freeze the assets of terrorists and those who support them, deny terrorists access to the international financial system, protect legitimate charities from being abused by terrorists, and prevent the movement of terrorists' assets through alternative financial networks.

However, this campaign need not be sequential to be effective, the cumulative effect across all regions will help achieve the results we seek. We will disrupt and destroy terrorist organizations by:

• direct and continuous action using all the elements of national and international power. Our immediate focus will be those terrorist organizations of global reach and any terrorist or state sponsor of terrorism which attempts to gain or use weapons of mass destruction (WMD) or their precursors;

• defending the United States, the American people, and our interests at home and abroad by identifying and destroying the threat before it reaches our borders. While the United States will constantly strive to enlist the support of the international community, we will not hesitate to act alone, if necessary, to exercise our right of self-defense by acting preemptively against such terrorists, to prevent them from doing harm against our people and our country; and

• denying further sponsorship, support, and sanctuary to terrorists by convincing or compelling states to accept their sovereign responsibilities. We will also wage a war of ideas to win the battle against international terrorism. This includes:

• using the full influence of the United States, and working closely with allies and friends, to make clear that all acts of terrorism are illegitimate so that terrorism will be viewed in the same light as slavery, piracy, or genocide: behavior that no respectable government can condone or support and all must oppose;

• supporting moderate and modern government, especially in the Muslim world, to ensure that the conditions and ideologies that promote terrorism do not find fertile ground in any nation;

• diminishing the underlying conditions that spawn terrorism by enlisting the international community to focus its efforts and resources on areas most at risk; and

• using effective public diplomacy to promote the free flow of information and ideas to kindle the hopes and aspirations of freedom of those in societies ruled by the sponsors of global terrorism.

While we recognize that our best defense is a good offense, we are also strengthening America's homeland security to protect against and deter attack. This Administration has proposed the largest government reorganization since the Truman Administration created the National Security Council and the Department of Defense. Centered on a new Department of Homeland Security and including a new unified military command and a fundamental reordering of the FBI, our comprehensive plan to secure the homeland encompasses every level of government and the cooperation of the public and the private sector.

This strategy will turn adversity into opportunity. For example, emergency management systems will be better able to cope not just with terrorism but with all hazards. Our medical system will be strengthened to manage not just bioterror, but all infectious diseases and mass-casualty dangers. Our border controls will not just stop terrorists, but improve the efficient movement of legitimate traffic.

While our focus is protecting America, we know that to defeat terrorism in today's globalized world we need support from our allies and friends. Wherever possible, the United States will rely on regional organizations and state powers to meet their obligations to fight terrorism. Where governments find the fight against terrorism beyond their capacities, we will match their willpower and their resources with whatever help we and our allies can provide.

As we pursue the terrorists in Afghanistan, we will continue to work with international organizations such as the United Nations, as well as non-governmental organizations, and other countries to provide the humanitarian, political, economic, and security assistance necessary to rebuild Afghanistan so that it will never again abuse its people, threaten its neighbors, and provide a haven for terrorists.

In the war against global terrorism, we will never forget that we are ultimately fighting for our democratic values and way of life. Freedom and fear are at war, and there will be no quick or easy end to this conflict. In leading the campaign against terrorism, we are forging new, productive international relationships and redefining existing ones in ways that meet the challenges of the twenty-first century.

U.S. Government, "National Security Strategy of the United States of America," September 2002, www.whitehouse.gov.

Document 9: Four Principles of U.S. Policy on Terrorism

The excerpt below is taken from the annual report on terrorism issued by the U.S. State Department. The document explains the fundamental principles of the Bush administration when dealing with terrorism.

President Bush has laid out the scope of the war on terrorism. Four enduring policy principles guide our counterterrorism strategy:

First, make no concessions to terrorists and strike no deals.

The US Government will make no concessions to individuals or groups holding official or private US citizens hostage. The United States will use every appropriate resource to gain the safe return of US citizens who are held hostage. At the same time, it is US Government policy to deny hostage takers the benefits of ransom, prisoner releases, policy changes, or other acts of concession.

Second, bring terrorists to justice for their crimes.

The United States will track terrorists who attack Americans, no matter how long it takes. This was demonstrated again in September 2001, when the United States arrested Zayd Hassan Abd al-Latif Masud al-Safarini, one of the chief perpetrators of the murderous hijacking in 1986 of Pan Am 73 in Karachi, Pakistan. He will stand trial in the United States for crimes committed during that brutal attack in which twenty-two persons—including two US citizens—were killed, and at least 100 persons were injured. Al-Safarini is the fourteenth international terrorist suspect arrested overseas and brought to the United States to stand trial since 1993. Others included Ramzi Yousef and Mir Aimal Kansi.

Third, isolate and apply pressure on states that sponsor terrorism to force them to change their behavior.

Libya is one of seven designated state sponsors of terrorism. Since the bombing of Pan Am 103 over Lockerbie, Scotland in 1988, the United States and Great Britain have pursued the Libyan perpetrators and sought to bring them to justice. In January 2001, a Scottish court convicted Libyan intelligence service member Abdel Basset al-Megrahi of the murder of 270 persons in connection with the Pan Am 103 attack. The court concluded that there was insufficient evidence to convict another Libyan defendant in the case. On 14 March 2002, a Scottish appellate court upheld Megrahi's conviction.

Fourth, bolster the counterterrorist capabilities of those countries that work with the United States and require assistance.

Under the Antiterrorism Assistance program, the United States provides training and related assistance to law enforcement and security services of selected friendly foreign governments. Courses cover such areas as airport security, bomb detection, hostage rescue, and crisis management. A recent component of the training targets the financial underpinnings of terrorists and criminal money launderers. Counterterrorist training and technical assistance teams are working with countries to jointly identify vulnerabilities, enhance capacities, and provide targeted assistance to address the problem of terrorist financing. At the same time special investigative teams are working with countries to identify and then dry up money used to support terrorism. We are also developing workshops to assist countries in drafting strong laws against terrorism, including terrorist financing. During the past 17 years, we have trained more than 35,000 officials from 152 countries in various aspects of counterterrorism. . . .

A broad range of counterterrorism training resources from other US Government agencies, including military training by the Department of Defense, is being brought to bear to bolster international capabilities. We will work with the world community and seek assistance from other partner nations as well.

U.S. State Department, "Patterns in Global Terrorism—2001," released May 21, 2002, www.state.gov.

Document 10: Building a Coalition Against Terror

Testifying before the Congressional Committee on International Relations, Secretary of State Colin Powell outlined the building of a coalition against terror. The secretary maintained that the coalition is necessary in order to fight terrorists with military, financial, and intelligence methods.

I would like to thank this Committee, and frankly the entire Congress, for the support that you have provided to the President's efforts since the 11th of September. It means a great deal to us. And not only that, it sends a signal to the world that we are unified. We are unified under President Bush's leadership. We are unified to pursue those who are responsible for the tragic events of September 11th. That day is seared against all of our souls. It is a day that we will never forget. But we came out of that day with a deep resolve to make sure that those who are responsible for that day will pay for it and be brought to justice. As the President said, they will have justice brought to them.

To that end, the President has undertaken a campaign to go after them. It is a campaign that has many dimensions to it: financial attacks, law enforcement attacks, intelligence attacks, military attacks. It is a campaign that is being waged not only by the United States but by the broad international coalition that has come together. And the reason this coalition has come together so quickly and so successfully is that everybody who has joined this coalition realizes that what happened in the United States on the 11th of September, and especially what happened in New York, was not just an attack against America, it was not just an attack against New York, it was an attack against civilization, it was an attack against the world community.

Some 80 nations lost citizens in the World Trade Center. And all of those nations have joined us in the counterattack, the campaign to go after those responsible.

But the President understood right away, within 24 hours, that it could not just be a campaign against the perpetrators, who are clearly the al-Qaeda organization led by Osama bin Laden, it had to be against all forms of terrorism. It had to be a broad-based campaign that brought all of the Members of the international community together, once and for all, to go after this scourge that exists on the face of the Earth, this scourge that is targeted against civilization, this scourge that is targeted against the democratic way of life, the democratic way of doing things.

It has nothing to do with Muslims. It is an attack against who we are, our value systems, our belief in the dignity of the individual, our belief in democracy, our belief in the free enterprise system. That is what it is an attack against.

It is not an attack that was delivered against us in the name of faith. It is a violation of the faith of Islam, it is a violation of every known faith that any man or woman believes in. We must not let Osama bin Laden make this false claim. We cannot also let him make the claim that somehow he is doing it in the name of the Palestinian people or Muslims. He lifted not a finger, he gave not a dollar of the wealth that he had to help his fellow Muslims or help the people who are suffering in the Middle East. Instead, he used his money for the worst sorts of purposes: to go out and murder innocent civilians. We must not let him get away with delivering a message that is different from that simple message.

As the President has said, he is an evil-doer. He must be punished as an evil-doer. And there are many terrorist organizations around the world that are similarly motivated, and we have to go after them wherever we find them.

And I now come to the fact that we put this rather incredible coalition together. There are some who said, well isn't the coalition a burden? Doesn't the coalition in some way contravene the President of the United States? The answer? The coalition does not constrain him in the slightest. As we pulled this coalition together, we made sure that the President retained all of his constitutional authority. Obviously, when you have a coalition, you have to be considerate of all of the interests of all of the members of the coalition. But in being considerate of the interests of all of the members of the coalition, the President in no way gave away any of his authority to act as he saw fit and may see fit in the future to protect American interests.

Second point with respect to the coalition. Without this coalition, we wouldn't be able to wage this campaign, we wouldn't be able to conduct this war. If we are to go after the financial systems of these organizations, you can't do it just by yourself. You need all of the nations that have financial systems that are relevant to come into this coalition so we can work together. If you are going to go after the intelligence infrastructure that he uses and get inside of that intelligence system, then you have to use all of the intelligence systems of the coalition members.

If you want to deliver a military strike against Osama bin Laden and al-Qaeda and the Taliban regime, you need a coalition to do that. You need people who will go into battle with you. You need people who will give you overflight. You need people who will support you. And the President has been absolutely marvelous, in my judgment, in pulling such a coalition together.

I will make one final point on this coalition. It was hard to stop it. Once people saw what happened on the 11th of September, they weren't just sitting around waiting for us to beg them to come into a coalition arrangement. Within 24 hours they had acted, invoking Article 5. Within 48 hours the U.N. had acted, passing a Security Council resolution, and then a General Assembly resolution.

As we really got ourselves mobilized, they came in one after the other, the Washington Treaty invoked, the Rio Pact invoked, organizations around the world wanting to be a part of this, the OAS [Organization of Atlantic States], and recently the Organization of the Islamic Conference, 56 Islamic nations coming together just 2 weeks ago.

We were worried about whether the Islamic conference would come out with something that might be troublesome for us. Instead they came out with a strong powerful statement that said what Osama bin Laden's associates did on the 11th of September was wrong, was representative of no faith, was not representative of the faith of Islam, was a desecration, and they understood the necessity for action against such terrorists and such kinds of activity.

"U.S. Diplomatic Efforts in the War Against Terrorism," Hearing Before the Committee on International Relations, House of Representatives, October 24, 2001, www.house.gov.

Document 11: Central Asian Nations Fight Against Terrorism: Declaration of Bishkek Conference on Security in Central Asia

On December 13 and 14, 2001, the Organization for Security and Cooperation in Europe sponsored a summit meeting of the countries of Central Asia, including Russia and observers from Western nations. The summit, held in Bishkek, Kyrgyzstan, dealt with the issue of terrorism, as these countries were now front line states in the battle against al-Qaeda terrorists based in Afghanistan. Below is the declaration agreed to at the conference.

The States participants of the international conference in Bishkek:

Resolutely condemning terrorism in all its forms and manifestations;

Acknowledging the primary role of the United Nations in the fight against terrorism and supporting resolutions no. 1377 (2001), 1373 (2001), 1368 (2001) and 1269 (1999) of the UN Security Council, as well as General Assembly Resolution 56/1 as a basis and framework for global co-operation to counter international terrorism;

Reaffirming the "Decision on Combating Terrorism" and the "Bucharest Plan of Action for Combating Terrorism" adopted at the Ninth Meeting of the Organization for Security and Cooperation in Europe (OSCE) Ministerial Council on 3–4 December 2001 in Bucharest;

Acknowledging the importance of the Declaration by the Central Asian states and the document "Priorities for Co-operation to Counter Drugs, Organized Crime and Terrorism in Central Asia", as endorsed in Tashkent, 20 October 2000;

Committed to address political conflicts and economic and social problems which are exploited by terrorists and violent extremists to mobilise support for their cause. Determined to translate their political will into action by joining forces to combat terrorism in all its forms and manifestations.

• Note the importance and timeliness of the Bishkek Conference 2001, as an international forum to strengthen understanding and share approaches in the struggle against terrorism.

• Emphasise that terrorism is a global problem and that there must be no safe haven for perpetrators of such crimes and their accomplices. It is a complex challenge due to links with transnational organized crime, illicit drugs, trafficking in human beings, money laundering, arms trafficking, computer and other high technology crimes as well as other threats, including the proliferation of weapons of mass destruction.

• Reject firmly the identification of terrorism with any particular religion or culture as well as the unacceptable attempts by terrorists and violent extremists to present their cause as a struggle between religions or cultures.

• Confirm that the struggle against terrorism requires joint and comprehensive efforts of the international community, in full conformity with the purposes and principles of the UN Charter, their obligations under international law, and the OSCE commitments they have undertaken, which closely link the OSCE's politico military, human and economic dimensions.

• Express their determination to combat terrorism while fully respecting human rights and the rule of law.

• Underline their commitment to address at the earliest possible moment political conflicts and economic and social problems which are exploited and abused by terrorists and violent extremists to mobilise support for their destructive causes.

• Call upon the international community, governments and civil societies to closely co-operate in the struggle against acts of terrorism in all its forms and manifestations on bilateral, regional and multilateral levels.

• Note that as a neighbor to Afghanistan, the Central Asian region is exposed to specific challenges and threats to security; in this connection, they note the contribution of the states in the region to the global coalition against international terrorism, and emphasized the necessity to render political support and financial/technical assistance to the states of Central Asia in this context, including support for sustainable development.

• Endorse the attached "Programme of Action", to initiate practical measures aimed at preventing and countering terrorism.

• Express their gratitude to the Government of the Kyrgyz Republic for having taken the initiative for this conference and for the excellent conference framework and hospitality in Bishkek.

This declaration was agreed amongst OSCE participating States represented at the conference on the basis of interventions made at the conference.

Declaration of the Bishkek International Conference on Enhancing Security and Stability in Central Asia: Strengthening the Comprehensive Efforts to Counter Terrorism, Bishkek, Kyrgyz Republic, December 13–14, 2001, http://usinfo.state.gov.

Document 12: Nurturing the Desire for Freedom and Democracy Around the Globe

In this excerpt from a speech, Henry Hyde, chairman of the House Committee on International Relations, argues that the United States must use "public diplomacy" in the war against terror. Public diplomacy involves stressing American values like freedom and democracy and communicating directly to ordinary people around the world to support the U.S. fight against terror.

My point is this: Our focus on our relations with foreign governments and international organizations has led us to overlook a set of powerful allies: the peoples of the world.

Uniquely among the world's powers, a dense network connects the United States with the populations of virtually every country on the planet, a network that is independent of any formal state-to-state interaction. On one level, this is not surprising: as the pre-eminent political, military, and economic power, the presence of the United States is a daily fact of life in most areas of the globe. America's cultural impact is even broader, penetrating to the most forbiddingly remote areas of the world, with a range continually expanded by the boundless reach of electronic media.

But there is an even deeper connection, a bond that derives from the universal values America represents. More than a simple wishlist of desirable freedoms, at their core is the belief that these values have universal application, that they are inherent in individuals and peoples by right of humanity and not by the grace of the powerful and the unelected. They provide hope even for those populations which have never experienced hope.

The advancement of freedom has been a prominent component of American foreign policy since this country's inception. Given the nature of the American people, it is certain to remain so.

But in addition to genuine altruism, our promotion of freedom can have another purpose, namely as an element in the United States' geopolitical strategy.

Despite the laments and exasperations of the practitioners of *Realpolitik* regarding what they see as our simplistic and naïve images of the world, we haven't done so badly. That virtually the entire continent of Europe is free and secure today is largely due to America's powerful and beneficent embrace, one that stretches unbroken from the landings in Normandy to the present day.

The history of the last century taught us many lessons, one of the most important being that the desire for freedom we share with others can be a remarkably powerful weapon for undermining geopolitical threats. The prime example is the Soviet Union.

Decades of enormous effort on the part of the United States and the West aimed at containing and undermining the threat posed by the Soviet empire enjoyed considerable success. But it was only with the advent of democracy in Russia and the other nations of the Soviet prisonhouse that the communist regime was finally destroyed and with it the menace it posed to us and to the world as a whole. This should be a deep lesson for us, but it is one that curiously remains unlearned by many.

Henry Hyde, "Speaking to Our Silent Allies: The Role of Public Diplomacy in U.S. Foreign Policy," June 15, 2002, www.house.gov.

Document 13: The Axis of Evil

The first presidential State of the Union Address after September 11, 2001, will be known for the phrase "axis of evil." President Bush used that phrase to describe those nations that he believed support terrorists, specifically Iraq, Iran, and North Korea. In this excerpt, Bush vows to pursue terrorists, disrupt their plans, and strike at them before they can strike at America. This "Bush Doctrine" of preemptive attack became controversial in the weeks following the speech.

Our nation will continue to be steadfast and patient and persistent in the pursuit of two great objectives. First, we will shut down terrorist camps, disrupt terrorist plans, and bring terrorists to justice. And, second, we must prevent the terrorists and regimes who seek chemical, biological or nuclear weapons from threatening the United States and the world.

Our military has put the terror training camps of Afghanistan out of business, yet camps still exist in at least a dozen countries. A terrorist underworld—including groups like Hamas, Hezbollah, Islamic Jihad, Jaish-i-Mohammed—operates in remote jungles and deserts, and hides in the centers of large cities.

While the most visible military action is in Afghanistan, America is acting elsewhere. We now have troops in the Philippines, helping to train that country's armed forces to go after terrorist cells that have executed an American, and still hold hostages. Our soldiers, working with the Bosnian government, seized terrorists who were plotting to bomb our embassy. Our Navy is patrolling the coast of Africa to block the shipment of weapons and the establishment of terrorist camps in Somalia.

My hope is that all nations will heed our call, and eliminate the terrorist parasites who threaten their countries and our own. Many nations are acting forcefully. Pakistan is now cracking down on terror, and I admire the strong leadership of President Musharraf.

But some governments will be timid in the face of terror. And make no mistake about it: If they do not act, America will.

Our second goal is to prevent regimes that sponsor terror from threatening America or our friends and allies with weapons of mass destruction. Some of these regimes have been pretty quiet since September the 11th. But we know their true nature. North Korea is a regime arming with missiles and weapons of mass destruction, while starving its citizens.

Iran aggressively pursues these weapons and exports terror, while an unelected few repress the Iranian people's hope for freedom.

Iraq continues to flaunt its hostility toward America and to support terror. The Iraqi regime has plotted to develop anthrax, and nerve gas, and nuclear weapons for over a decade. This is a regime that has already used poison gas to murder thousands of its own citizens—leaving the bodies of mothers huddled over their dead children. This is a regime that agreed to international inspections—then kicked out the inspectors. This is a regime that has something to hide from the civilized world.

States like these, and their terrorist allies, constitute an axis of evil, arming to threaten the peace of the world. By seeking weapons of mass destruction, these regimes pose a grave and growing danger. They could provide these arms to terrorists, giving them the means to match their hatred. They could attack our allies or attempt to blackmail the United States. In any of these cases, the price of indifference would be catastrophic.

We will work closely with our coalition to deny terrorists and their state sponsors the materials, technology, and expertise to make and deliver weapons of mass destruction. We will develop and deploy effective missile defenses to protect America and our allies from sudden attack. And all nations should know: America will do what is necessary to ensure our nation's security.

We'll be deliberate, yet time is not on our side. I will not wait on events, while dangers gather. I will not stand by, as peril draws closer and closer. The United States of America will not permit the world's most dangerous regimes to threaten us with the world's most destructive weapons.

Our war on terror is well begun, but it is only begun. This campaign may not be finished on our watch—yet it must be and it will be waged on our watch.

George W. Bush, State of the Union Address, January 9, 2002, www.whitehouse.gov.

Document 14: Reforming the Department of Justice

Attorney General John Ashcroft describes new legislation and reforms of the FBI designed to increase security following September 11, 2001.

Ten months ago, our nation came under attack. In a calculated, deliberate manner, terrorists slammed planes into the World Trade Center, the Pentagon, and a field in Pennsylvania, killing thousands. These attacks were acts of war against our nation, and an assault on the values for which we stand—the values of equality, justice, and freedom. This unprecedented assault brought us face to face with a new enemy, and demanded that we think anew and act anew in order to protect our citizens and our values.

Immediately following the attacks, I ordered a top-to-bottom review and reorganization of the Department of Justice. Our objective was to mobilize the resources of our law enforcement and justice system to meet a single, overarching goal: to prevent future terrorist attacks on the United States and its citizens.

The review found that America's ability to detect and prevent terrorism has been undermined significantly by restrictions that limit the intelligence and law enforcement communities' access to, and sharing of, our most valuable resource in this new war on terrorism. That resource is information. . . .

Based on this review, we concluded that our law enforcement and justice institutions—and the culture that supports them—must improve if we are to protect innocent Americans and prevail in the war against terrorism. In the wake of September 11, America's defense requires a new culture focused on the prevention of terrorist attacks. We must create a new system, capable of adaptation, secured by accountability, nurtured by cooperation, built on coordination, and rooted in our Constitutional liberties.

Congress has already taken the first, crucial steps to adapt to our changing security requirements.

The passage of the USA-PATRIOT Act made significant strides toward fostering information sharing and updating our badly outmoded information-gathering tools. The Patriot Act gave law enforcement agencies greater freedom to share information and to coordinate our campaign against terrorism. Prosecutors can now share with intelligence agents information about terrorists gathered through grand jury proceedings and criminal wiretaps. The intelligence community now has greater flexibility to coordinate their anti-terrorism efforts with our law enforcement agencies.

The Patriot Act also modernized our surveillance tools to keep pace with technological change. We now have authority under FISA to track terrorists who routinely change locations and make use of multiple cell phones. Thanks to the new law, it is now clear that surveillance tools that were created for hard line telephones—pen registers, for instance—apply to cell phones and the internet as well.

The recently announced reorganization of the Federal Bureau of Investigation is a second way we have risen to meet the new challenges we face. Our reorganization comes in the midst of the largest criminal investigation in United States history, and the expansion of FBI-led Joint Terrorism Task Forces to each of the 56 FBI field offices. Our reorganization refocuses the FBI on a terrorism prevention mission that is different from the past. Instead of being reactive, agents will now be proactive. Instead of being bound by rigid organizational charts, our work force will become flexible enough to launch new terrorism investigations to counter threats as they emerge.

Management and operational cultures will be changed to enhance this adaptability. Over 500 field agents will be shifted permanently to counter-terrorism. Subject matter experts and historical case knowledge will be centralized so they are accessible to field offices, the intelligence community, and our state and local law enforcement partners.

The counter-terrorism division at FBI headquarters will be restructured and expanded significantly to support field offices and other intelligence and law enforcement organizations. And finally, we will enhance the FBI's analytical capacity and integrate our activities more closely with the CIA.

A third way in which we have acted to enhance our homeland security is by giving updated guidance to our FBI agents in the field. After a meticulous review of the previous Attorney General's guidelines, which unnecessarily inhibited agents from taking advantage of new information technologies and public information sources, revised guidelines were announced in May. These new directions to FBI agents are crafted carefully to correct the deficiencies of the old guidelines, while protecting the privacy and civil liberties of all Americans.

Throughout this reform process, the Department of Justice has been guided by four values—the four principles that shape and inform our new anti-terrorism mission: Adaptability. Accountability. Cooperation. Coordination. By following these lodestars, we have worked with Congress and our partners in law enforcement to correct the excesses of the past and to achieve a more stable, secure equilibrium in our justice policy. The creation of the Department of Homeland Security will prove critical to this process of restoring balance to our security policy.

John Ashcroft, Statement Before the Committee on the Judiciary, U.S. Senate, July 25, 2002, www.usdoj.gov.

Document 15: Intelligence Failures and September 11

In testimony before a Joint Session of the House and Senate Committees on Intelligence, an anonymous FBI agent describes how "the wall" of seperation between various agencies and offices led to the intelligence failures that allowed the September 11 attacks to occur.

I am a Special Agent of the Federal Bureau of Investigation (FBI) assigned to the New York Field Office. I appreciate your invitation to appear before your Committees today in connection with your Joint Inquiry into the tragic events of September 11, 2001. I fully understand the responsibility with which you have been charged. I intend to cooperate with you and answer your questions to the best of my ability.

I am speaking to you today as an individual agent. The views I express, therefore, are my own, not necessarily those of the FBI, although I believe that my concerns are shared by many fellow agents. I hope by appearing here today I might help in a small way to assure that the men and women of the FBI and others in the Intelligence Community, have access to the information necessary to carry out their sworn duty to protect the people of the United States.

I have no wish in the remarks that follow to be critical of any person. Whether they are at (FBI) Headquarters or in the field, FBI personnel work their hearts out to perform our mission. I am before you today to address practices that frustrate us all. Much has been written about how the FBI does not share information with local law enforcement agencies, but the American people must realize that the FBI does not always have access to the information itself, nor is all information the FBI possesses available to all of its agents. It is my belief that the former problem is due to fear that the Bureau may "run ahead" or "mess up" a current or future operation of one of our sister agencies—and the latter primarily due to decisions that have snowballed out of the Foreign Intelligence Surveillance Act (FISA) Court. A concept known as

"The Wall" has been created within the Law Enforcement and Intelligence Communities. From my perspective, and in its broadest sense—"The Wall" is an information barrier placed between elements of an intelligence investigation and those of a criminal investigation. In theory—again same perspective—it is there to ensure that we, the FBI, play by the rules in our attempts to gather evidence in a criminal case and Federal prosecution.

I have tried to write this statement knowing full well that its contents and my testimony will be studied by the enemy. Along those lines—much detail has been left out and if I may, humbly remind everyone that questions regarding sources, other possible operations, and investigative methods in this forum should be approached with extreme caution.

As an aside, may I say I firmly believe prevention is best served by allowing the Law Enforcement Community—Federal and local—to conduct sound, sometimes exigent investigations, with access to all information that the US Government and Liaison Governments possesses. These investigations build sources, evidence, connections and information—and are not simply reactive. I would like to assure the American people that in my almost seven (7) years in the Bureau, the FBI has always been in the Prevention—if I may—"Game".

Before going further, I would like to offer a few words of introduction so that you are aware of the background that I bring to the questions before the Committees. Between 1985 and 1993, I served in the military. After a brief stint in the private sector, I joined the FBI in December 1995, and was assigned to the New York Field Office's Joint Terrorism Task Force in July 1996. From July 1996 through October 1997, I worked on the TWA Flight 800 investigation. In October 1997, I was assigned to the squad that had responsibilities for Taliban and Pakistan matters. Following the East Africa Embassy bombings in August 1998, I was part of the first team on the ground, spending a cumulative total of over 30 weeks abroad investigating the bombings.

In early 1999, I joined the New York Field Office's Usama bin Laden (UBL) case squad, which is responsible for the overall investigation of UBL and Al-Qaeda. Immediately after the attack on the USS *Cole* in Aden, Yemen on October 12, 2000, I was assigned as one of the case agents and worked on that case—Adenbom—until the attacks of September 11, 2001. Since then I have also worked on general UBL matters and have been deployed 12 weeks overseas, working along side other Intelligence Community components. I mention this fact because, although there are issues about the sharing of information with FBI investigators by the CIA—my experience is the FBI and the Intelligence Community have worked successfully together. The people of the United States should take great pride in the service and sacrifice of the men and women of all the US Agencies and DOD deployed overseas—many of whom I have had the privilege of working with overseas.

Briefly, "The Wall," and implied, interpreted, created or assumed restrictions regarding it, prevented myself and other FBI Agents working a criminal case out of the New York Field Office from obtaining information from the Intelligence Community, regarding Khalid Al-Mihdhar and Nawaf Al-Hazmi in a meeting on June 11, 2001. At the time, there was reason to believe that Al-Mihdhar and Al-Hazmi had met with a suspect connected to the attack against the USS *Cole*. The situation came to a head during the fourth week of August 2001, when, after it was learned that Al-Mihdhar was in the country, FBI HQ representatives said that FBI New York was compelled to open an "intelligence case" and that I nor any of the other "criminal case" investigators assigned to track Al-Qaeda could attempt to locate him. This resulted in a series of e-mails between myself and the FBI HQ analyst working the matter.

In my e-mails, I asked where this "The New Wall" was defined. I wrote on August 29, 2001: "Whatever has happened to this—someday someone will die—and wall or not—the public will not understand why we were not more effective and throwing every resource we had at certain 'problems'. Let's hope the National Security Law Unit will stand behind their decisions then, especially since the biggest threat to us now, UBL, is getting the most 'protection.'" I was told in response that "we [at headquarters] are all frustrated with this issue," but "These are the rules. NSLU does not make them up."

I hope, Messrs. Chairmen, these proceedings are the time to break down the barriers and change the system which makes it difficult for all of us, whether we work at FBI HQ or in the field, at the FBI or elsewhere, to have and be able to act on the information that we need to do our jobs.

Anonymous FBI Agent, "Testimony Before the House and Senate Select Committees on Intelligence," September 20, 2002, www.fbi.gov.

Document 16: The War on Terror and the Expansion of Federal Power

Always on the lookout for the expansion of government power into the lives of ordinary Americans, maverick legislator Ron Paul saw this dan-

ger in the aftermath of September 11. Polls showed that many Americans were willing to give up rights for security. The Texas congressman worries that Americans will lose hard won rights in the attempt to gain more security.

The events of September 11th understandably made Americans far more concerned about their safety here at home. All of us want action taken to diminish the threat of future terrorist attacks, and President Bush is doing a very good job of pursuing bin Laden and his cohorts overseas. The proper focus should be on identifying those responsible and using limited military force to bring them to justice. We should arrest or kill the perpetrators abroad, use our armed forces more wisely to defend our borders, and reform immigration laws to keep terrorists out.

Unfortunately, the focus in Congress seems to be on a domestic agenda that will adversely affect millions of ordinary Americans without making us any safer. An example can be found in a Customs Service bill slated for a vote in the House. This bill gives customs and postal agents new authority to open and inspect outgoing U.S. mail without probable cause or a warrant. I don't think many Americans are comfortable with having federal agents open and search the mail they send! Of course it's easier to pass such a measure when the public is in a fearful mood and demanding action. Ten or twenty years from now, when the recent attacks are a distant memory, federal agents will still be opening mail—mail sent by American citizens, not terrorists.

Americans face an internal threat every bit as dangerous as foreign terrorists: the loss of domestic freedoms. Every 20th century crisis—two great wars and a decade-long economic depression—led to rapid expansions of the federal government. The cycle is always the same, with temporary crises used to justify permanent new laws, agencies, and programs.

The cycle is repeating itself. Congress has been scrambling to pass new legislation (and spend billions of your tax dollars) since September [2001]. Most of the new laws passed and dollars spent have nothing to do with defending our borders and cities against terrorist attacks. I have already written and spoken at length concerning the dangers to our civil liberties posed by the rush to pass new laws. I do not believe that our Constitution permits federal agents to monitor phones, mail, or computers without a warrant. I do not believe that government should eavesdrop on confidential conversations between attorneys and clients. I certainly do not believe "terrorism" should be defined so broadly that American citizens expressing dissent against their own government could be investigated and prosecuted as terrorists.

Remember, President Bush will not be in office forever. History demonstrates that the powers we give the federal government today will remain in place indefinitely. How comfortable are you that future Presidents won't abuse those powers? Politically-motivated IRS audits and FBI investigations have been used by past administrations to destroy political enemies. It's certainly possible that future executives could use their new surveillance powers in similarly unethical ways. The bottom line is that every American should be very concerned about the unintended consequences of policies promoted to fight an unending, amorphous battle against terrorism.

Ron Paul, "Terrorism and the Expansion of Federal Power," December 10, 2001, www.house. gov.

Document 17: The President's Remarks to the Nation on the Anniversary of the September 11 Attacks

On the aniversary of the World Trade Center and Pentagon attacks, President George W. Bush addressed the nation from Ellis Island, New York. The president honored those lost in the attacks and praised those who sacrificed in the war on terror. He pledged that the United States would fight to extend freedom and democracy around the world.

THE PRESIDENT: Good evening. A long year has passed since enemies attacked our country. We've seen the images so many times they are seared on our souls, and remembering the horror, reliving the anguish, re-imagining the terror, is hard—and painful.

For those who lost loved ones, it's been a year of sorrow, of empty places, of newborn children who will never know their fathers here on earth. For members of our military, it's been a year of sacrifice and service far from home. For all Americans, it has been a year of adjustment, of coming to terms with the difficult knowledge that our nation has determined enemies, and that we are not invulnerable to their attacks.

Yet, in the events that have challenged us, we have also seen the character that will deliver us. We have seen the greatness of America in airline passengers who defied their hijackers and ran a plane into the ground to spare the lives of others. We've seen the greatness of America in rescuers who rushed up flights of stairs toward peril. And we continue to see the greatness of America in the care and compassion our citizens show to each other.

September 11, 2001 will always be a fixed point in the life of America. The loss of so many lives left us to examine our own. Each of us was reminded that we are here only for a time, and these counted days should be filled with things that last and matter: love for our families, love for our neighbors, and for our country; gratitude for life and to the Giver of life.

We resolved a year ago to honor every last person lost. We owe them remembrance and we owe them more. We owe them, and their children, and our own, the most enduring monument we can build: a world of liberty and security made possible by the way America leads, and by the way Americans lead our lives.

The attack on our nation was also attack on the ideals that make us a nation. Our deepest national conviction is that every life is precious, because every life is the gift of a Creator who intended us to live in liberty and equality. More than anything else, this separates us from the enemy we fight. We value every life; our enemies value none—not even the innocent, not even their own. And we seek the freedom and opportunity that give meaning and value to life.

There is a line in our time, and in every time, between those who believe all men are created equal, and those who believe that some men and women and children are expendable in the pursuit of power. There is a line in our time, and in every time, between the defenders of human liberty and those who seek to master the minds and souls of others. Our generation has now heard history's call, and we will answer it.

America has entered a great struggle that tests our strength, and even more our resolve. Our nation is patient and steadfast. We continue to pursue the terrorists in cities and camps and caves across the earth. We are joined by a great coalition of nations to rid the world of terror. And we will not allow any terrorist or tyrant to threaten civilization with weapons of mass murder. Now and in the future, Americans will live as free people, not in fear, and never at the mercy of any foreign plot or power.

This nation has defeated tyrants and liberated death camps, raised this lamp of liberty to every captive land. We have no intention of ignoring or appeasing history's latest gang of fanatics trying to murder their way to power. They are discovering, as others before them, the resolve of a great country and a great democracy. In the ruins of two towers, under a flag unfurled at the Pentagon, at the funerals of the lost, we have made a sacred promise to ourselves and to the world: we will not relent until justice is done and our nation is secure. What our enemies have begun, we will finish.

I believe there is a reason that history has matched this nation with this time. America strives to be tolerant and just. We respect the faith of Islam, even as we fight those whose actions defile that faith. We fight, not to impose our will, but to defend ourselves and extend the blessings of freedom.

We cannot know all that lies ahead. Yet, we do know that God had placed us together in this moment, to grieve together, to stand together, to serve each other and our country. And the duty we have been given—defending America and our freedom—is also a privilege we share.

We're prepared for this journey. And our prayer tonight is that God will see us through, and keep us worthy.

Tomorrow is September the 12th. A milestone is passed, and a mission goes on. Be confident. Our country is strong. And our cause is even larger than our country. Ours is the cause of human dignity; freedom guided by conscience and guarded by peace. This ideal of America is the hope of all mankind. That hope drew millions to this harbor. That hope still lights our way. And the light shines in the darkness. And the darkness will not overcome it.

May God bless America.

George W. Bush, "President's Remarks to the Nation," September 11, 2002, www.whitehouse. gov.

Discussion Questions

Chapter 1: Events Leading Up to September 11

1. Do U.S. policies lead to conflict between the United States and Muslims? If so, which policies cause the most conflict between America and the Islamic world?

2. Were the September 11 attacks a response to U.S. actions or simply the acts of militant fanatics using outrage over American policies as a rationale to commit senseless mayhem? Defend your answer with references to the readings.

3. What alternative policies can the United States pursue to promote peaceful coexistence between Islam and the Western world?

Chapter 2: Debating the War on Terrorism

1. Is the United States morally justified in using military force to combat terrorism? Why or why not?

2. Can democracy and human rights be imposed by force in the Middle East? Explain your answer.

3. What would a victory in the war against terrorism look like? How will America know when it has won?

Chapter 3: Domestic Antiterrorism Efforts

1. Do current domestic antiterrorism efforts hurt civil liberties in the United States? If so, in what way?

2. Which government agency, in your opinion, is the key to success in the war against terrorism in the United States? What are this agency's most effective tools in combatting terrorism?

3. Benjamin Franklin is supposed to have said, "Those who would trade liberty for security deserve neither liberty nor security." Do you think Franklin would have the same opinion today after the September 11 attacks? Would he think Americans have given up too much freedom? Explain.

Chapter 4: The Next Phase: How Should the War Proceed?

1. What military tools are most effective against terrorism? Is our current military structure suited to the war against terrorism? Why or why not?

2. Who is the true enemy in the war against terror? Will the United States fight against all terrorist groups with equal effort? If so, is the United States capable of fighting all terrorist groups at once? If not, which terrorist groups (other than al-Qaeda) will be the United States's primary targets?

3. Is the cooperation of Islamic nations truly necessary in the war against terror, or is the United States strong enough to "go it alone"? If cooperation is necessary, how can the United States go about building the necessary alliances with the Islamic world?

4. What will be the reaction of Islamic governments and peoples to U.S. troops being based in or near their countries? Will such a U.S. presence lead to more or fewer terrorist incidents? Why?

5. Do you believe the United States should use military force to depose Iraqi leader Saddam Hussein? Why or why not?

Chronology

1989
Osama bin Laden founds an international terrorist group known as al-Qaeda (the Base).

April 1991
Saudi Arabia expels Osama bin Laden; he takes up residence in Sudan.

February 26, 1993
A bomb in a van explodes in the underground parking garage in New York's World Trade Center, killing 6 people and wounding 1,042.

April 1994
Saudi Arabia strips Osama bin Laden of his citizenship for his antimonarchical activities.

1996
The Central Intelligence Agency (CIA) sets up a special unit to track Osama bin Laden's activities. Sudan offers to turn bin Laden over to the United States or Saudi Arabia, but both countries refuse the offer. The United States lacks evidence to indict bin Laden.

May 18, 1996
Sudan expels Osama bin Laden; he moves to Afghanistan.

June 25, 1996
A bomb aboard a fuel truck explodes outside a U.S. Air Force installation in Dhahran, Saudi Arabia. Nineteen U.S. military personnel are killed in the Khobar Towers housing facility; more than 370 others are wounded.

September 27, 1996
The Taliban seizes Kabul, the capital of Afghanistan. After seizing power, the fundamentalist rebels impose a harsh version of Islamic law on the Afghan population.

January 8, 1998
Ramzi Yousef, an associate of Osama bin Laden, is sentenced to life without parole for orchestrating the 1993 World Trade Center bombing.

February 22, 1998
Osama bin Laden issues an edict calling for attacks on American citizens.

August 7, 1998
Terrorist bombs destroy the U.S. embassies in Nairobi, Kenya, and Dar es Salaam, Tanzania. In Nairobi, 12 Americans are among the 291 killed, and over 5,000 are wounded, including 6 Americans. In Dar es Salaam, one U.S. citizen is wounded among the 10 killed and 77 injured.

August 20, 1998
The United States attacks targets in Afghanistan and Sudan in retaliation for the U.S. embassy bombings in Africa. Over seventy-five cruise missiles are fired from U.S. Navy ships in the Arabian and Red Seas. Most strike six separate targets in a camp near Khost, Afghanistan. About twenty cruise missiles strike a factory in Khartoum, Sudan, which is suspected of producing components for making chemical weapons.

1998–1999
A U.S. grand jury indicts Osama bin Laden for the bombing of the U.S. embassies in Africa.

October 12, 1999
A covert operation to send sixty Pakistani commandos to Afghanistan to capture or kill Osama bin Laden is aborted when a military coup overthrows Pakistani prime minister Nawaz Sharif.

October 12, 2000
The U.S. Navy destroyer USS *Cole* in the Yemeni port of Aden is attacked by terrorists linked to Osama bin Laden; the attack kills seventeen crew members and injures forty-two.

December 19, 2000
The UN Security Council (UNSC) unanimously adopts a resolution demanding that the Taliban government abides by UN Security Council Resolution 1267 by turning Osama bin Laden over to a country where he can be brought to justice, closing all terrorist training camps in Afghanistan, and complying with other UNSC demands.

May 29, 2001
A U.S. district court finds four of Osama bin Laden's followers guilty of conspiring to kill Americans, including those killed in the U.S. embassy bombings in Africa.

September 11, 2001
Terrorists hijack four U.S. commercial airliners taking off from various locations in the United States in a coordinated suicide attack. In separate attacks, two of the airliners crash into the twin towers of the World Trade Center in New York City, which catch fire and eventually collapse. A third airliner crashes into the Pentagon in Washington, D.C., causing extensive damage. The fourth airliner, also believed to be heading toward Washington, D.C., crashes outside of Shanksville, Pennsylvania, killing all forty-five people on board. Casualty estimates from New York put the possible death toll close to three thousand, and nearly two hundred people died at the Pentagon crash site.

September 12, 2001
President George W. Bush meets with his national security advisers and with leading members of Congress. He also telephones the leaders of Great Britain, Canada, France, Germany, China, and Russia as the first steps toward building an international coalition against terrorism. He calls the attacks "acts of war" and announces that he will ask Congress for additional funds to protect the nation's security.

September 14, 2001
President Bush orders the mobilization of up to fifty thousand National Guard and Reserve personnel for port operations, medical and engineer support, and homeland defense. The Defense Department plans to mobilize thirty-five thousand from all services. Congress authorizes President Bush to use all necessary military force against the perpetrators of the September 11 attacks, their sponsors, and those who protect them. The Senate approves the resolution by a vote of 98 to 0; the House of Representatives' vote is 420 to 1. The House and Senate also unanimously approve a supplemental spending bill authorizing up to $40 billion for disaster relief, counterterrorism, and military operations.

September 18, 2001
In Afghanistan, Taliban leader Mohammed Omar refuses a Pakistani demand to surrender Osama bin Laden and calls a meeting of Muslim clerics to decide bin Laden's fate. As Taliban leaders urge their countrymen to prepare for a holy war with the United States, thousands flee Afghan cities. Pakistan attempts to close its border to stem the flood of refugees.

September 25, 2001
Defense Secretary Donald Rumsfeld announces the start of Operation Enduring Freedom, the military phase of the war against terrorism.

September 27, 2001
The White House announces an extended aviation security plan. The plan includes an expanded air marshals plan and $500 million to fund modifications to aircraft to prevent hijackings. President Bush also announces that he will work with Congress to federalize airport security operations throughout the nation.

September 28, 2001
The UNSC unanimously adopts Resolution 1373, which establishes wide-ranging measures to combat terrorism, especially focusing on the financial support terrorists need to carry out their acts.

October 7, 2001
President Bush announces that the U.S. military has launched strikes against al-Qaeda terrorist camps and Taliban military installations in Afghanistan.

October 8, 2001
North Atlantic Treaty Organization (NATO) secretary-general Lord Robertson states that NATO ambassadors have expressed their full support for the actions of the United States and the United Kingdom against al-Qaeda installations that began on October 7. President Bush establishes the Office of Homeland Security, which is charged with coordinating the domestic security efforts in the United States; he appoints former Pennsylvania governor Tom Ridge as director.

October 11, 2001
President Bush holds his first prime-time news conference. He tells the Taliban government that if it gives up bin Laden and his followers, "we'll reconsider what we're doing to your country." He also says that the United States is prepared to help the UN establish a stable and representative Afghan government that would be involved in neither terrorism nor the drug trade.

October 19, 2001
U.S. Special Forces enter Afghanistan for the first time. They coordinate their activities with the Northern Alliance.

October 22, 2001
Homeland Security director Tom Ridge announces that two Washington, D.C., area postal workers have tested positive for inhalation of anthrax. In addition, two postal workers die of suspected anthrax infection. Anthrax spores are also found at a post office in Trenton, New Jersey.

October 25, 2001
The U.S. Treasury Department creates Operation Green Quest, aimed at eliminating terrorists' money sources. The operation seizes the assets of organizations that raise money for terrorist operations and investigates currency smuggling and money laundering.

October 26, 2001
President Bush signs the USA Patriot Act into law, expanding the power of the federal government to gather information by means of wiretapping and other techniques.

October–November 2001
The United States and other Western powers provide air power and Special Forces assistance to help the Afghan Northern Alliance defeat the Taliban.

November 1, 2001
Acting on FBI information, California governor Gray Davis announces that a "credible threat" exists of a terrorist attempt to destroy a major bridge in California between November 2 and 7. No attack occurs, and no arrests are made.

November 11–12, 2001
Northern Alliance forces take Kabul, the Afghan capital.

November 22, 2001
The Taliban government surrenders the city of Kunduz, a major stronghold in northern Afghanistan.

November 25, 2001
The "American Taliban," John Walker Lindh, is captured by anti-Taliban forces in Afghanistan and is held at a prison near Mazar-e Sharif, where he is questioned by CIA agents. When Taliban prisoners revolt later that day, Walker Lindh is shot in the thigh and takes refuge in a basement. He surrenders on December 1, 2001, and is subsequently questioned, charged with engaging in terrorist acts, convicted, and sentenced to twenty years in federal prison.

December 7, 2001
The Taliban forces flee Kandahar, their last major stronghold in Afghanistan. Osama bin Laden's whereabouts remain unknown.

December 12, 2001
President Bush signs into law legislation to help provide health and educational assistance to the women and children in Afghanistan and in refugee camps in neighboring countries.

December 13, 2001
The Defense Department releases a videotape of Osama bin Laden discussing the September 11 terrorist attacks against the World Trade Center and the Pentagon; the video was believed to have been taped in Kandahar in mid-November. The tape shows bin Laden saying that the devastation caused by fuel-laden jetliners crashing into the twin towers far exceeded his expectations.

December 19, 2001
The Department of Transportation sets hiring standards for new baggage and passenger screeners. The new rules require the screeners to be U.S. citizens and pass background and criminal record checks.

December 20, 2001
International peacekeeping forces arrive in Afghanistan.

December 22, 2001
Richard Reid, a British Muslim, tries to blow up American Airlines Flight 63, flying from Paris to Miami, by means of explosives in his shoes. Passengers prevent Reid from carrying out the attack.

January 12, 2002
The first group of al-Qaeda prisoners lands at Guantanamo Bay, Cuba. The U.S. Department of Defense holds the prisoners in Cuba in order to avoid possible legal actions if they are brought to the United States. There is international criticism over treatment of the prisoners and the fact that they are being held with uncertain legal status. The Defense Department wishes to hold the prisoners indefinitely in order to conduct interrogations and ensure that they will not engage in terrorism in the future.

January 29, 2002
President Bush delivers his annual State of the Union address, in which he describes Iraq, Iran, and North Korea as an "axis of evil" because they promote terrorism. U.S. policy, according to Bush,

will be to make sure that these states are not able to produce weapons of mass destruction that can be transferred to terrorists for attacks on the United States.

February 4, 2002
President Bush announces that the Homeland Security budget will include $3.5 billion for "first responders" such as firefighters, police officers, and paramedics. Other expenditures include $11 billion—a $2 billion increase—for better border security and $700 million for improving intelligence collecting and sharing.

March 20, 2002
Director Ridge announces the Homeland Security Advisory System (HSAS). The system is designed to provide the public with information on the terrorist threat. The possible activities of terrorist groups are evaluated according to available intelligence, and the Department of Homeland Security then issues an advisory to the public as to the level of threat. According to the system, there are five levels of terrorist threat, ranging from low risk of terrorist activity (green) to severe risk of terrorist activity (red).

July 25, 2002
Zacarias Moussaoui, the so-called twentieth hijacker, appears in federal court on charges relating to the September 11 attacks. Moussaoui, a French citizen of Moroccan heritage, had been arrested on August 17, 2001. However, FBI investigators were not able to obtain a court order to search Moussaoui's computer, which contained data that linked him to the plot, until after the September 11 attacks.

September 19, 2002
President Bush calls on the United Nations to act on a resolution to ensure that Iraq disarms and allows weapons inspectors to carry out proper inspections of possible weapons-making facilities. Bush says that the United Nations's credibility is at stake, and if the international organization does not act, the United States will.

September 20, 2002
The White House announces the new National Security Strategy for the United States, a large part of which is concerned with the war against terrorism. The document sets forth the so-called Bush Doctrine, the policy of striking at terrorists before they can strike at targets in the United States.

October 6, 2002
A French oil tanker is attacked off the coast of Yemen; Islamic militants are suspected of carrying out the attack.

October 7, 2002
President Bush outlines the Iraqi threat in a speech in Cincinnati, Ohio. Bush says that Iraq, under Saddam Hussein, has a history of aggression, has supported terrorism, and is trying to develop weapons of mass destruction. The speech is intended to influence a congressional vote authorizing the use of military force against Iraq.

October 10, 2002
A strong bipartisan majority in Congress authorizes President Bush to use force against Iraq.

October 12, 2002
Two bombs rip through a packed discotheque on the Indonesian island of Bali, killing more than two hundred people and injuring some three hundred. Most of those who died were young people, many of them Australians. Islamic terrorists are suspected.

October 25, 2002
The FBI warns of a possible terrorist attack against transportation facilities, particularly railroads. The information that led to the warning came from al-Qaeda prisoners, who warned of plans to attack bridges and other key points of the U.S. transportation system.

November 3, 2002
Six suspected al-Qaeda members are killed in Yemen in a rocket attack launched from an unmanned U.S. aircraft.

November 8, 2002
After months of negotiations, the UNSC approves a resolution calling on Iraq to either disarm and allow inspectors into its facilities or "face force," in the words of British prime minister Tony Blair. The resolution, which passed by a 15 to 0 vote, frees the United States to attack Iraq without further UN authorization.

For Further Research

Books

As'ad AbuKhalil, *Bin Laden, Islam, and America's New "War on Terrorism."* New York: Seven Stories, 2002.

Robert Baer, *See No Evil: The True Story of a Ground Soldier in the CIA's War on Terrorism.* New York: Crown, 2002.

John V. Blane, ed., *Cyberwarfare: Terror at a Click.* Huntington, NY: Novinka Books, 2001.

David A. Charters, ed., *The Deadly Sin of Terrorism: Its Effect on Democracy and Civil Liberty in Six Countries.* Westport, CT: Greenwood, 1994.

John K. Cooley, *Unholy Wars: Afghanistan, America, and International Terrorism.* London: Pluto, 2000.

Anthony H. Cordesman, *Terrorism, Asymmetric Warfare, and Weapons of Mass Destruction: Defending the U.S. Homeland.* Westport, CT: Praeger, 2002.

Joseph D. Douglass, *America the Vulnerable: The Threat of Chemical and Biological Warfare.* Lexington, MA: Lexington Books, 1987.

Rohan Gunaratna, *Inside Al Qaeda: Global Network of Terror.* New York: Columbia University Press, 2002.

Nadine Gurr and Benjamin Cole, *The New Face of Terrorism: Threats from Weapons of Mass Destruction.* London: I.B. Tauris, 2000.

Colbert C. Held, *Middle East Patterns: Places, Peoples, and Politics.* Boulder, CO: Westview, 2000.

Harry Henderson, *Global Terrorism: The Complete Reference Guide.* New York: Checkmark Books, 2001.

Philip B. Heymann, *Terrorism and America: A Commonsense Strategy for a Democratic Society.* Cambridge, MA: MIT Press, 1998.

Lawrence Howard, *Terrorism: Roots, Impact, Responses.* New York: Praeger, 1992.

Samuel Huntington, *Clash of Civilizations.* New York: Simon and Schuster, 1996.

Brian Michael Jenkins, *Countering Al Qaeda: An Appreciation of the Situation and Suggestions for Strategy.* Santa Monica, CA: Rand, 2002.

Walter Laqueur, *The New Terrorism: Fanaticism and the Arms of Mass Destruction.* New York: Oxford University Press, 1999.

David E. Lon, *The Anatomy of Terrorism.* New York: Free, 1990.

Richard F. Nyrop and Donald M. Seekins, eds., *Afghanistan, a Country Study.* Washington, DC: Headquarters of the Department of the Army, 1986.

David J. Whittaker, *Terrorism: Understanding the Global Threat.* London: Longman, 2002

———, ed., *The Terrorism Reader.* London: Routledge, 2001.

Paul L. Williams, *Al Qaeda: Brotherhood of Terror.* Parsippany, NJ: Alpha, 2002.

Periodicals

Jurgen Brauer, "On the Economics of Terrorism," *Phi Kappa Phi Forum*, Spring 2002.

David Brooks, "How Suicide Bombing Became Not Just a Means but an End," *Atlantic Monthly*, June 2002.

Frank J. Cillufo and Thomas Tomarchio, "Responding to New Terrorist Threats," *Orbis*, Summer 1998.

Daniel Dayan, "Media, the Intifada and the Aftermath of September 11," *European Judaism*, Spring 2002.

James X. Dempsey, "Counterterrorism and the Constitution," *Current History*, April 2000.

James Fallows, "The Unilateralist, an Interview with Paul Wolfowitz," *Atlantic Monthly*, March 2002.

Carol Graham, "Can Foreign Aid Help Stop Terrorism? Not with Magic Bullets," *Brookings Review*, Summer 2002.

Mark Juergensmeyer, "Understanding the New Terrorism," *Current History*, April 2000.

Walter Laqueur, "What to Read (and Not to Read) About Terrorism," *Partisan Review*, Summer 2002.

Mahmood Mamdani, "Good Muslim, Bad Muslim: A Political Perspective on Culture and Terrorism," *American Anthropologist*, September 2002.

Charles C. Mann, "Homeland Insecurity," *Atlantic Monthly*, November 2002.

John Newhouse, "The Threats America Faces," *World Policy Journal*, Summer 2002.

Barry Rubin, "The Real Roots of Arab Anti-Americanism," *Foreign Affairs*, November/December 2002.

David Schafer, "Islam and Terrorism: a Humanist View," *Humanist*, May/June 2002.

Kirsten E. Schluze, "Militants and Moderates," *World Today*, January 2002.

James Steinberg, "Counter Terrorism: A New Organizing Principle for American National Security?" *Brookings Review*, Summer 2002.

Cass R. Sunstein, "Why They Hate Us: The Role of Social Dynamics (Anti-Americanism and Group Polarization)," *Harvard Journal of Law and Public Policy*, Spring 2002.

John M. Swomley, "Parlaying Tragedy into Empire (Watch on the Right)," *Humanist*, September/October 2002.

Mary Anne Weaver, "Blowback," *Atlantic Monthly*, May 1996.

Elisabeth Young-Bruehl, "On the Origins of a New Totalitarianism," *Social Research*, Summer 2002.

Index

political objectives of, 131
  concerning U.S. Middle East
    policy, 16, 54, 80, 166
  support for, 11, 85
    from CIA during Soviet
      occupation of Afghanistan,
      67–68
    from Islamists worldwide, 147
    from Taliban, 13–14, 24, 34–35
    al-Qaeda leader, 10, 129
Bingham, Mark, 74
Black September terrorist group, 108
Blair, Tony, 11
Bodansky, Yossef, 10
bombings, 28, 32, 91, 110, 120
  in Bali, 16
  in Egypt, 32
  of Israeli embassy in Argentina,
    108
  in Lebanon, 39
  of New York World Trade Center
    (1993), 15, 26, 102, 103, 168
  of Pan Am Flight 103, 70
  of U.S. embassies in Kenya and
    Tanzania, 28, 31, 33–34, 37–40
  of U.S. military compound in
    Saudi Arabia, 16, 39
  of USS Cole, 16, 91
  see also September 11 attacks
Bosnia, 147, 158, 159
Boyd, John, 129–30
Britain, 11, 46, 147, 161
British Petroleum (oil company),
  46
Brzezinski, Zbigniew, 26, 48, 49, 68
Bush, George W., 12, 95, 113, 168
  good understanding of war on
    terrorism shown by, 59
  hypocrisy of, 66
  precipitous military action likely to
    be taken by, 65, 69
  response to September 11 attacks
    by, 67
Bush administration, 130, 135–36,
  154–55
  commercial interests of, 83, 85, 88
  diplomatic capacity shown by, 20
  lack of support for Iraqi resistance
    to Saddam Hussein and, 61
  obligations in Afghanistan and, 163
  responsibility to protect innocent
    people and, 70–71
  ultimatum given to Taliban by, 13

unilateralism of, 81
weakness of, 53–54
Butler, Richard, 167

Camden, Pat, 111
Cannistraro, Vincent, 124–25
Cantor Fitzgerald, 76–77
Carter, David, 116
Carter administration, 48
Casey, William, 24–25
Center for Constitutional Rights,
  112
Central Asia, 13, 25, 26, 82
  nature of Islam in, 161
  oil and natural gas in, 83
  U.S. diplomacy in, 20
  U.S. military bases in, 154, 162
    need to maintain long-term, 157
    to help weak states resist
      Islamic extremism, 159–60
    for stabilization of Afghanistan,
      163–64
    possible problems for U.S.
      resulting from, 155
    include complications in
      relationships with major
      powers, 156
Central Intelligence Agency (CIA),
  60, 62, 98, 169
  in Iran, 46
  role of, in creating Mujaheddin,
    24–25, 29
    growth of fundamentalist
      movement a result of, 32, 48, 85
    support for bin Laden a part of,
      67–68
  tracking of bin Laden by, 30
  training of state police for
    homeland security and, 110, 112
Chalabi, Ahmed, 60, 61
Chechnya, 98, 159
Chiapas Coalition, 112
Chicago, 103, 110
  police department of, 111
China, 90, 120–21, 155, 156
Cipro, 85
civil liberties, 67
  erosion of, 121, 139
    for detainees, 12, 86, 125–26
      falsely justified by label "enemy
        combatant," 119, 123
      falsely justified by need for
        security, 117, 122
    by Justice Department,115, 116